How the Supernatural Found Me

My Journey in the Spirit

By Fred Herzog

Edited by Hannah Vollmuth and Andrea Van Essen, book layout by Evan Mattsen, cover design by Max Mayrhofer and publishing services by Well Done Publishing

ISBN 978-1-7366274-1-9

Printed in the United States of America

To the Comforter and Helper:
Holy Spirit

Table of Contents

Introduction
Becoming a Soul-Winner for Christ

In the college setting, everything seems to come to life-or-death decision making because no one wants to ruin their life!

I imagined being a pastor someday, but I wondered about being able to lead songs for worship because every pastor in my church experience was the song leader as well. I noticed that whenever people were invited to sing Christmas carols, I ended up sweeping the floor or being asked to be helpful behind the scenes. I hadn't quite realized that I just could not sing or carry a tune. While in this state of confusion around vision and career-setting, an invitation came from my mother to come back home and meet a university professor who talked about "the great experiment" in the Holy Spirit.

Well, a home-cooked meal never hurt anyone, so I obliged and came home that Saturday night and stayed for church the next morning to hear this guy. His name was Fred Smith, and I was surprised to hear him speak about experiencing God on a basis that I never really knew before. I listened to his Sunday class, and then I stayed for the church service and talked to him later. After dinner that Sunday, I wondered if this British professor would allow me to come over to his house and visit with him.

I found his number and went to see him. When I got there, he was sitting in his big chair by the fireplace. He invited me in, and I asked about this great experiment that he was always talking about. It turned out it was all about being baptized in the Holy Spirit and receiving the power to witness. He challenged me, and I responded by inviting the Holy Spirit into my life with the expectation of receiving power to witness for Christ in a way that was unfamiliar to me. We just didn't do that kind of thing in the churches I attended.

I felt I needed to do something else, an act that later I was not too sure about—I wrote a contract with God. I promised that if I did not obey Him, He could take my life because I felt no real worth anyway.

That very day I went to the house of a colleague of mine, a fellow school bus driver, and asked to see him. His wife came to the door and said that he was taking a shower, so I told her I would wait. When he came to meet me, I began witnessing to him about Christ and told him that God wanted his life. He answered by telling me that he was not ready but that I was the third person that day who had told him the very same thing!

I went away discouraged but not defeated. Dr. Smith, who had become my new friend, also challenged me to witness every day and come to a 6:00 AM prayer meeting on Saturday mornings. I went and began to catch a vision for sharing Christ and began witnessing to people on my way to college. I lived about forty-five minutes from school and drove the bus in the morning and afternoons. I began leading people to Christ on a daily basis and would call up Dr. Smith every time someone came to Christ. After a while, he suggested I just give him a weekly call to tell him how many had come to Christ that week.

I found a book at the college library, and it spoke of a missionary who would pray and ask the Lord how many people should come to

Christ that next day. I said to myself, *If God could do that for him, why can't He do that same thing for me?*

From then on, my day consisted of going to school, driving the bus mornings and afternoons, and witnessing to anyone who would listen to me. I realized that the kids who sat around the bus driver could be witnessed to as well.

However, a problem began to develop because they asked questions about the Bible, but I didn't have time to teach them because I had to drive. So, we started Bible studies; but here another problem began to surface. Now they said that their churches did not and could not answer their questions, and they asked me if *I* could start a church.

Well, this was getting way too deep for me, but I later took all these things into consideration, and it led me to starting churches for the Lord.

Chapter One
Godly Beginnings

The calling of God in my life was emphatic! I was studying at Northwestern College in Minneapolis, Minnesota, and I was asking God about what He had in store for me. I couldn't sing—how could I be a good pastor without that skill? I read my personal devotions on a daily basis and came across this text in Jeremiah 1:4-5.

> Then the word of the LORD came unto me, saying, Before I formed thee in the belly I knew thee; and before thou camest forth out of the womb I sanctified thee, and I ordained thee a prophet unto the nations
>
> (King James Version)

With this Scripture in hand, I went to my mother who was the spiritual source in our family. I was so excited that God was speaking to me, that I could hardly wait to tell her. However, before I could finish getting the Scripture out of my mouth, she said, "Wait—I have something to tell you!"

She began telling me that when she was a young teenager, a cousin from Alabama came to visit her family in Mound, Minnesota. He got the whole family out on the farm lawn and preached Christ to them. At the end of his message, he challenged everybody to share the gospel.

His challenge was, "I have come all the way from Alabama to share the gospel of Christ with you; who of you will take the gospel to the world?"

This was probably the first time they had really heard the gospel, and my uncle stood up and said, "I will go!"

But my grandfather said, "Oh no you won't, you have to stay home and take care of the farm!"

So, my mother said to the Lord, "If You will allow me to get married and have a son, then I will give him to You to go to the world."

And so, she turned to me and said, "Fred, you are that son, and now God has confirmed it!"

She then explained that many times she would sit in her rocking chair and pray for that son of promise, reiterating to God that He could use her to birth a son who would be called to go into the world.

I didn't recognize the depth and importance of my mother's vow at the time, but I later discovered that it was a key ingredient in God's purpose and calling on my life. Over the years, several other pivotal incidents helped shape who I was to become, and one of those occurred in Waco Texas.

MY JOURNEY TO WACO, TX

A few months after getting married in 1966, the Lord challenged me to go to a church conference called The Grace Gospel Homecoming in

Waco, Texas. I told the Lord that I didn't really want to go. This conference was Pentecostal, so I was not interested.

Finally, I said "Okay, Lord. If you give me a gold Cadillac and free gas, then I will go."

I thought this was hard for God to do, but lo and behold, it all came about, and I knew I had to go.

Once I arrived in Waco, I immediately knew that this would be a different kind of experience. The power of God was moving, and people were being touched by the Lord. Just being in that atmosphere, I began to operate in the gifts of the Spirit in ways that were new to me. I was speaking to a college-age woman who was attending the conference, and without knowing it, I began to operate in the gift of the word of knowledge. I spoke into areas of her life that she had not told me about, and she was absolutely shocked. To my horror, she asked me if I had been spying on her! After trying to convince her for several minutes that those words just came out of my mouth and that it must have come from God, she proposed a test.

She said, "Well Fred, if you got those insights from God, then tomorrow tell me how to implement the words that you shared with me. If He gives you the answers for that, then I will know that you didn't spy on me."

With fear and trembling, I sought the Lord for the wisdom that I needed to share with her. To my relief, He came through, and she knew that God had spoken to her.

Having just come out of my first year of seminary, a conference like this felt like a rodeo! I didn't know what to expect or what would happen next. For example, one day I saw a commotion, and I went over to see what was happening. There was a man who had a goiter larger than my fist growing on the right side of his neck. He asked for prayer. The leader of the conference, Dad Ewing, prayed for him and the goiter completely disappeared! All that was left was a flap of skin hanging down where the goiter once was.

I was hit with fear, and the devil said to me, "Fred, look what happens! When you ask for prayer, they make you swallow it!"

I walked away not wanting any prayer because I didn't know what I would have to swallow!

On a different day, I was standing right next to Dad Ewing when I saw something strange. Several men were praying for another man who was absolutely ecstatic. He was walking in place and looked like he was going up an escalator that wasn't there. I got close to Dad Ewing and asked what was happening to that man over there.

Dad said, "Don't worry. He just has more of the anointing than he knows what to do with—he is simply letting it out."

Initially everything had seemed so wild, but after about four or five days, people were leaving the conference and I had calmed down. By this time, I had figured out that nobody was going to haul me away in a wagon like I had read about in Elmer Gantry. Still, I stayed as close as I could to Dad Ewing, not knowing what was going to happen next.

At one point, a middle-aged man came up to him and said, "Dad, I haven't been able to drive home to Oklahoma because I don't have any gas for my car. What should I do?"

Dad responded, "Young man, go find all the gas cans that you can. Once you have them, let me know."

At the time I thought to myself, *Sir, we just had 500 people here; why didn't you ask any of them for gas or money while they were still around?*

After several hours, that man came back and said that he had found all the gas cans that he could. He then led us to his station wagon.

Dad gathered others around and said, "We are going to pray for this brother's car. Everybody lay hands on it."

Being a good seminarian, I wanted to get in on the action—but not get too close—so I prayed for the headlights. Dad Ewing went back to the gas tank and asked for a funnel. As soon as he removed the gas cap, gasoline started spraying out of the car's tank!

He said, "Pass me a can!"

4

Once he had filled up all eight or nine of the gas cans that the man had collected, Dad had to force the gas cap back onto the tank because of the gas that was squirting out!

All he said was, "Brother, there you go; now you can get home."

Then everyone just walked away. I watched the man from Oklahoma put up the hatch of the station wagon. He then placed all the filled gas cans into his vehicle and drove off.

Although I soon drove home as well, I was a changed man after that trip. Over the years, I returned many times and eventually became a leader within the network that God established there. The spiritual DNA that came out of that group of believers in Waco had a lasting influence on the churches that God later allowed me to establish. The concept of the New Testament Church structure was a focal point of that group and was based out of the history of what God had done with those believers in Texas. Their story is a remarkable one.

NEW TESTAMENT CHURCH ORIGIN

This New Testament Church began in a little Presbyterian mission church in Waco, Texas in the early 1940s. Glenn Ewing, who was affectionately called Dad Ewing, was an elder in that church. The pastor of the church was Dr. Gear who was getting toward the age of retirement and was looking for a smaller church to end his career in. When his best options seemed to be to stay in Waco, he kept his house and maintained his retirement by starting a little mission church across town. He made the move and drew some fellow Presbyterians to join with him. This included Dad Ewing, who became an elder in that new mission church.

After a period of time, Pastor Gear developed gout in his body and was looking for a cure. He went to a healing meeting and ended up being healed and speaking in tongues. A few years later, he went to be with the Lord. During that time of sickness, he had appointed Dad

Ewing to be the pastor if anything happened to him. Dad Ewing was a cashier in a local bank. Once the pastorate fell to him, he began to seek God about what to do as pastor because he had not received any formal education in the ministry. His decision was to begin to study the book of Acts and to follow it.

If the early church operated according to the book of Acts, what better way could there be than to pattern this mission church after it? It was not long before some of the members of the congregation began to express concerns that they were not remaining Presbyterian. When their concerns were not addressed, and the mission church continued to follow the book of Acts, many of the members returned to the main Presbyterian church where they had come from. This left Dad Ewing with a small congregation and a fresh desire to follow what the early New Testament church was experiencing. They were not yet acquainted with healing, speaking in tongues, fasting, or being bold in their witness as part of their Christian life.

At this time, the believers who met with Dad Ewing were looking for fellowship and trying to identify with other believers, and they shared some of the same values and experiences that they were learning about. Through this reaching out, word got to a man who lived in England named Bishop Jardine. He was an early Pentecostal apostle who had started many churches under the outpouring of the Spirit in the 1904 revival that had spread from Wales to England. The revival in England had since subsided, and most of the early ministries had been absorbed into the Church of England. Still, Bishop Jardine had a deep yearning for the Lord to help him start just one more church before he died. He was invited to come to the United States to perform a wedding, and he heard about the quest of this little mission church in Waco.

He went and visited them, preached, and shared his desire with them to set one more church into divine order. If they were interested, then they would have to fast for three days to prepare for his coming and to be ready to allow the Holy Spirit to work. He told them that in every church that he had set into divine order, a demon-possessed woman would fall on the floor, act like a snake, foam at the mouth, and try to take over the church. However, after the demon was cast out, she would then become a good Christian worker in the church.

He stayed and taught them every night for a week. He asked them to consider whether they wanted him to set their church into divine order and to give him an answer when he returned after doing the wedding. The church decided to take the challenge and fast for three days. They had never fasted before, and they were unfamiliar with the various types of fasts recorded in the Bible—so they fasted three days without food or water in the hot Texas weather. God was with them, and they survived and decided to have Bishop Jardine come and set the church in divine order.

He came and taught three times a day for ten days. During this time of setting the church in order, a lady had a demonic manifestation in the exact way that he had described. Her name was Sister Hoppi. I met her and had fellowship with her, and she had become a wonderful Christian worker for the church.

This humble beginning set the stage for a worldwide impact that is still being felt today. The principles, teachings, and examples of these early New Testament Church pioneers have now reached even to you. Countless individuals have been trained or influenced by this group of believers, and their ministries have touched nearly all the continents of the world. Some of the key people were Bobby Martz, Ray Jennings, Earl Kellum, Wayne Crooke, James Cooper, Carlton Kenney, Ray Brooks, and Robert Ewing. As far as I know, I am the last remaining apostle from that original group that is still in ministry. All the rest have gone home to be with their Lord.

The main doctrinal emphasis was being in divine order, the divine order truths, living by faith, moving in the Spirit, the grace message, five-fold ministry, and the biblical structure and order for the New Testament Churches in our generation. These teachings were radically new to me when I first encountered them in the 1960s. Given that I didn't live in Texas at the time, I needed a place closer to home where I could grow in these new dimensions of the Spirit. God opened up just such a place through a ministry called Daystar.

DAYSTAR: A PLATFORM TO GROW

In these early days of learning to minister, the Holy Spirit was teaching me new principles and ways of God on a regular basis. Often new insights came out of praying into situations that I didn't have answers for. However, because many churches were still not open to the expressions of the Holy Spirit, it became increasingly important to find and grow with believers who were. One day, I discovered this fellowship group called Daystar. Here I learned more extensively about prophecy, operating in the words of knowledge, and even deliverance. It was so amazing to me that God could actually use me in this way. I was involved with teaching and ministering at Daystar off-and-on for several years. So, here is a little background about the Daystar Ministry group.

Daystar Ministries was a communal ministry center for people who had been filled with the Spirit but had no opportunity for the expression of their gifts in their local churches. In the late 1960s, people were finding the move of the Holy Spirit and were sensing the need to come together and identify with other like-minded believers. The founder of Daystar Ministries was Jack Winter. He had a Lutheran heritage and went to St. Olaf College, where he prayed for God to work. He joined Bethany Fellowship and learned the communal lifestyle and incorporated it into a ministry center.

This was a time when pastors were being removed from their churches and denominations and needed a place to belong and learn about the new release of the Spirit. Those who joined Daystar would sell their houses or put their life savings into the ministry as a loan. That money was then used to purchase retreat properties which eventually became the Daystar Ministry Center. Daystar emphasized worship, deliverance, and a retreat ministry for people to get away for personal growth. This ministry center is where I was able to find the opportunity to function in the gifts of the Spirit and develop in the spiritual arena. The tools and experience that I gained in that setting proved foundational for doing personal ministry. They were also necessary skills when I started my first church.

PLANTING A DIVINE ORDER CHURCH

New Testament Church was my very first attempt at establishing a divine order church, which began on April 30th, 1970. It started with a small group of people who wanted to please God and initiate something that featured divine order. People were tired of the denominational structure that we all had been a part of in our former churches. A small group of around thirty people, mostly college students, working young adults, and some older parents of children who had been touched by God, joined together to form this unorthodox church.

It focused on Christ's challenge to the church (Matthew 28:18-20), Christ's ministry through the church (Luke 4:18), and Christ's discipleship model (Luke 6:40; 14:26, 27, 33). This group also had a vision to create a fellowship of people where body ministry and the gifts of the Holy Spirit were free to operate. Hearing from God, personal ministry, and deliverance were a major part of the church life.

People from all denominational backgrounds attended, and many received the changed life that they were looking for. Witches were set free, homosexuals were delivered, bones and teeth were healed, and marriages were restored. A spiritual authority rested on the church in such a measure that demonic curses were broken, people controlled by demons were delivered, and individuals were set free to serve God.

This church soon grew and became a major player in the charismatic fellowship of churches in the Twin Cites Metro. A vision to create sister churches was soon voiced, and as a result, over a dozen congregations were formed in the outlying areas. These churches often began when young people in our church got married or got jobs in different communities and had to move. Often, they didn't find new churches where they lived that were like the one that they had left. So, they would call me up and ask if a church like the one in Eden Prairie could be started in their community as well. These churches were circling the Twin Cities and eventually began to develop in foreign countries as well. From this church, many were led to go into full-time ministry and are still serving the Kingdom of God as this book is being written.

After seven years of being the apostle, senior pastor, and founder of the church, I was challenged by the Lord to release the people so that they would put their trust fully in Jesus Christ and not have a wrong dependence on the church father. This was a major change for everyone, and the men who were being trained up were then able to take the responsibility of caring for the church from there. The church and the subsequent network of churches were later released into their care, and they have taken on different characteristics as the times and seasons have changed.

Chapter Two
Learning to Live on the Street

I was enrolled in Trinity Seminary in the Chicago area and went to go get started in my seminary education only to find out that it was for the next year. After coming home to my wife with this great news, she promptly said,

"You're not going to wait until next year and sit around; so go, get a job."

Well, the job that opened up was being a youth pastor at the Edgewater Covenant Church in Chicago. The average age in the church was sixty-seven, and it was my responsibility to invite young people to come and make this church grow. I was to receive one hundred dollars a week to grow a youth group from around the church area. Instead, I discovered several gangs, and they were not made up of church-going kids. These kids enjoyed playing games with the authorities by robbing the meat market across the street and having the cops chase them for excitement. Besides sniffing glue and sitting down on the Foster Pier on Lake Michigan, they were having sex after school. I soon realized that I needed to memorize at least one kid's name in each gang in case I was in trouble and needed to get okayed by some member of the gang. Here I was, an Excelsior boy from Minnesota, learning the rules of how to stay alive on the Chicago streets.

Ministering on the streets was never a dull affair. One day, a young man was drunk, and as I prayed for him, he became completely sober. That same day, another student in the area had a dog bite and said, "Man, is this Jesus able to heal dog bites?" I prayed for him as well, but I never heard anything more from him. However, the brother of that kid heard about what had happened and came to see us. His name was Mike, and he actually asked for prayer. Now, this was big stuff on the street where God was operating. Kids there didn't just come up asking to be prayed for. Well, Mike was trying to stop smoking but could not quit, so he was willing to take a chance and be ministered to. I prayed and asked God to make smoking taste like burnt rags in his mouth. The prayer was answered, and he could not smoke any more as a result.

The leadership of the church wanted me to go visit the families of the kids in the hope of having them come to the church. Well, my first visit was to a kid's family named Kallus. He lived in an apartment building in the area, and when I went into the building, I did not know that I should not have had an overcoat and dress hat on as I entered the building. As I entered, every door on the floor slammed shut and I was alone in the place.

I went to the door where Kallus, his dad and his brother lived. I found a man dying from not being able to breathe. He wanted to know about his kid and how he was doing. When I told him that he was down at the pier sniffing glue instead of being in school, it did not sit real well with him. So, when I got back to the church office the next day, all the kids of the neighborhood were sitting on the front steps of the church telling me what this kid was going to do to me for getting his dad mad at him for not going to school. I did not realize that I broke a gang rule of snitching on someone.

Well, the penalty for this was to have your lower lip slit with a knife and be scarred for life as a snitch. Alternatively, I could be beaten up and dropped through a manhole into the street sewer, along with all the alligators that people flush down the toilets when they were no longer pets for their kids.

I had just dropped Charlotte off for church one evening and located a parking place for our blue Ford Mustang Convertible, when I heard a voice from behind me telling me all the things that were going to happen to me for snitching on him to his father.

My thoughts were, *God, unless You do something, Charlotte is going to be a widow. Lord it is up to You because this is out of my hands right now.* I knew that kid carried a 14-inch butcher knife, and it would go right through the convertible's canvas, into my shoulder blades, and I would be dead. But thanks be to God and the Holy Spirit who entered me at that time and all fear left me. I commanded that kid to get to my office and we would go to church together.

As this was happening, the gifts of the Holy Spirit began to operate, and I had words of knowledge and wisdom of what to do. I told him to open the church door, but he said that he was unable to get the door open. I did not believe him until I saw that his hand could not reach or grasp the door. So, I opened the door and took him and his sidekick along up to the crying room on the 2nd floor, because he would scare the people in church. While in the crying room, his skin color changed from beige to brown and black around his nose. The next thing I heard was chairs moving around, and the other kid, who was holding him down, said, "Preacher, you have to watch while you pray. Don't close your eyes." After seeing that he had demonic activity operating in him, I asked God what demons they were, and I was told hate and murder. Not knowing what to do, I told them to leave in Jesus' name, and they left. Then He became born again and we ended our conflict.

13

Ed, a friend of my brother-in-law Scott, took me out to coffee to tell me something important. He began sharing about the baptism of the Holy Spirit and about speaking in tongues, and I attentively listened to him for an hour and a half. After he had finished his oration, I informed him that I didn't believe a word of it. He in turn told me that I was incorrigible. When Scott found out about this, he insisted that it was absolutely necessary for me to be baptized in the Holy Spirit.

I said, "You have tongues; I have visions. You keep yours, and I will keep mine."

At the time, my brother-in-law Scott attended Faith Tabernacle, a church in Chicago where people regularly testified to their changed lives that resulted from receiving the baptism in the Holy Spirit, including overcoming drug addiction. He really wanted me to receive the baptism as well. So, he changed his approach. He told me to lie down on the floor, breathe in and breathe out, and then I would be enabled to receive the Holy Spirit. He had received the Holy Spirit in a similar manner, that is why he had faith in this unorthodox approach.

Obediently, I inhaled and exhaled on the floor, but didn't feel any different. Under Scott's continual inquiries of whether I had received the baptism, I finally stood up and said, "Hey! I got it!". While I didn't notice an initial shift, I would soon find out that God had used that opportunity to change me.

Following this floor exercise, I ran into an odd situation on the street. A man with demonic issues was trying to give his girlfriend pills used for mating horses. Apparently, he had acquired them from another individual off the street. As bizarre as this situation was, what took place next was perhaps even more shocking to me. When I took this man up to my office to pray for him, I started speaking in a language that I had never known before! Amazingly, the demons started leaving him when I spoke these funny new words. I decided to look up praying in tongues in the Scriptures, and after finding it, I decided to accept the baptism of the Holy Spirit.

Chapter Three
How God Calls Someone

At various points in my Christian walk, I had significant experiences that either altered my trajectory in life or changed who I was to become. While God was always involved in this process of change, I often only later understood the extent of His involvement and the gravity of the transformation. These turning points were more than just lessons or encounters; they were facets of God's calling on my life.

THE CALL TO BE A MENTOR

My call to mentoring began through a friend at Northwestern College named Al Moir, who was just out of the Marines. One morning while waiting for classes to start, he asked, "Does anyone want to be a part of a Bible study?" There was a fellow from the Air Force, and there was me. When the Air Force guy declined, I said I would be glad to be part of this study. Well, I found out it was more than a Bible study—it was a mentoring study on how to change people's lives.

Al had been mentored and trained by The Navigators, a discipleship-based ministry group started by Dawson Trotman. So, Al became my mentor, and we had the objective to study every week and share what God showed us. This was stretching for me because even though I was a believer and wanted to hear from God, I was not in a place where He spoke to me every day. I was also invited to a weekly Bible study and had to invest a certain number of hours in order to attend. It was disciplined. This principle of mentoring has meant so much to me that I decided to mentor others in the same way that I was mentored.

After many years of training others, I have developed four basic goals that I aim to accomplish in my mentoring relationships. The first is to create confidence in people's God-given call and giftings. The second is to help in the development and implementation of the dreams that people have. This is what I have done with my wife and each of my three children. The third is to cultivate the leadership qualities in each person being mentored. Finally, the fourth is to help people discover the underdeveloped issues in their lives in order for them to grow in maturity.

Hebrews 13:7 is a Scripture passaged that speaks so well of the mentoring process and sheds light on the qualities of a mentor that one should look for. I am just going to list them for simplicity's sake.

Six Indicators for Finding the Right Mentor

1. One who has a sense of destiny
2. One who cares for and accepts people
3. One who accepts responsibility
4. One who recognizes another as a leader
5. One who inspires others
6. One who leads by example

The Word of God must be the foundation for the mentoring process. Additionally, a genuine mentor needs to operate in transparency. You cannot reproduce after your own kind in a mentoring context unless the person you are mentoring can see who you really are. How can someone duplicate your walk without knowing the heart and character that are behind it?

I have enjoyed the privilege of being able to mentor many people for the Kingdom of God. Some have been businessmen, some have been those aspiring to be pastors, and still others have been those who just wanted to have their lives be more productive. As a result of this calling, I have had many successes and a few that did not turn out as well as I had hoped. In conclusion, I would like to offer my own definition of mentoring. Mentoring is an opportunity to engage in the development, construction, and operation of a person and their worldview by sharing your knowledge, wisdom, and life experiences as an encouraging life guide to help them fulfill the destiny that they were created to walk in.

THE CALL TO COUNSELING

God calling me into counseling was a considerable challenge because of how He spoke to me. The church that I was involved in had a founding brother, and his wife reached out to me for marriage counseling. Now, I knew that she had been married more years than I was old, so to say that I felt inadequate is an understatement. My mind went into a panic, and I said, "God what can I do? I am not prepared to meet this challenge!"

I prayed that she would not come for counseling—mostly out of fear and my wanting to avoid possible relational problems. But the Lord spoke to me and said that if I would trust Him, He would not work by the educational process I had learned in school, nor by my experience, but by the gifts of the Spirit and the principles of the Word of God.

I agreed to those terms, and He began to show me how this was going to work. He said that He would bring people to me with needs and problems that I had never even heard of before, but not to be afraid because He would give me the word of knowledge in regard to their problems. Then, after I would come to a place of recognizing the principle, He would give me the word of wisdom for the situation.

I was told that this would be like a course in counseling. Once I had learned that particular means of dealing with a problem, then He would bring people with a new problem, and we would start all over again with the word of knowledge and wisdom. This process became so successful that, at times, the Lord would have me tell people coming for counseling what their question or problem was before they could even share it. This was possible because God allowed me to see it written on their foreheads.

This caused many to be amazed and created faith, because they would of course ask, "How did you know that?"

My answer from the Lord was that if God, who loved them so much, could tell them about their issue through another person, then He certainly could heal them too! Many, many people were set free through this method of counseling. I have kept all those notes and have put them into a counseling course that I have used to train many people.

THE APOSTOLIC CALL

The apostolic call of God in my life was more than I could imagine. Growing up, I had been shy, reserved, and generally lacked confidence. In my grade school days, I was afraid to go to school because the teacher called me dumb and said that I would never amount to anything. To even think that God could use me was a stretch of my imagination, so when the Lord had already started two churches through me, it was more than I could believe. However, when a brother said that he thought I was an apostle, I could not entertain the idea. My idea of apostles was old men with long beards, and even apart from that, they probably did not exist in this church age! I was challenged to look into the Scriptures to find out just what the purpose and time for apostles in the church was. Ephesians 4:7-13 spoke to this most clearly:

> But unto each one of us was the grace given according to the measure of the gift of Christ. Wherefore he saith, When he ascended on high, he led captivity captive, And gave gifts unto men. (Now this, He ascended, what is it but that he also descended into the lower parts of the earth? He that descended is the same also that ascended far above all the heavens, that he might fill all things.) And he gave some to be apostles; and some, prophets; and some, evangelists; and some, pastors and teachers; for the perfecting of the saints, unto the work of ministering, unto the building up of the body of Christ: till we all attain unto the unity of the faith, and of the knowledge of the Son of God, unto a fullgrown man, unto the measure of the stature of the fulness of Christ
>
> (American Standard Version)

I also found a Biblical Greek scholar at Moody Bible School who offered some insights regarding apostles. He defined an apostle as, "One sent on a commission to represent another person, the person sent being given credentials and the responsibility of carrying out the orders of the one sending him."[1] I realized that in Ephesians 4:7-13 the

---

[1] Kenneth S. Wuest, *Romans in the Greek New Testament* (Grand Rapids: Wm. B. Eerdmans Publishing Company, 1955), p.12.

person doing the sending is Christ, and He deposits part of Himself in that apostolic individual that he sends on a mission.

It was interesting to discover that no human being actually makes you an apostle, but God does. In his writings, Paul often referenced the source of his apostolic credentials, particularly at the beginning of his letters. He wrote that he was an apostle based on calling (1 Corinthians 1:1), based on the will of God (Ephesians 1:1), and based on appointment (1 Timothy 2:7). I also learned that apostles can be tested (Revelation 2:2). It began to make sense how churches would get started because of the unique ministry of the apostle. After looking through the Scriptures, I realized that this ministry has seven aspects to it.

The Ministry of the Apostle

1. The church overseer and designer
    1 Cor. 3:10-15
2. The church foundation layer
    Eph. 2:17-20
3. The church structural overseer
    1 Cor. 12:28; Titus 1:5
4. The church trainer
    Corporate – Acts 19:8-10
    Individual – Acts 16:1-5
5. The church team player/leader
    Five-fold ministry is Christ's team – Eph. 4:11
    Close team worker is the prophet – Eph. 2:20; 1 Cor. 12:28
    Local team – Acts 20:17-38
6. The signs of an apostle
    2 Cor. 12:12
7. The sufferings of an apostle
    1 Cor. 4:9-13; 2 Cor. 1:6; 2 Tim. 3:10-12

After much research, I was amazed to find out that the total number of apostles mentioned in Scripture, as well as the reality of present-day apostles, was different than I had thought. As a result, I did a complete about-face on the subject. By this time in my study, others whom I respected talked about apostles and prophets as well. So, I began to pray in earnest whether I could actually be operating in an apostolic capacity. It is still overwhelming to me all these years later, when I look back at the struggles and the fruit of starting over thirty churches with my wife. But God has proven the reality of present-day apostles.

Of course, the apostle is not the only ministry that is given as a gift by Christ to his church. The apostle needs to cooperate with the other ministries mentioned in the fourth chapter of Ephesians in order for the Body of Christ to grow into health and maturity. For example, we read in Ephesians 2:20 that the apostles and prophets work together to lay foundations. We also see in 1 Corinthians 12:28 that there is an order and an authority structure involved for the various ministries and gifts to work together.

I began to understand that the Holy Spirit could shift me into any of the ministries of Christ that He had anointed me to function in. He showed me that it was like shifting a manual stick shift in a car. I was to shift into whichever gear was most needed in the particular church that I was ministering in. For example, if a church had a pastor and an apostolic leadership, then I would operate in the prophetic role at that church, to fill in what was missing. Knowing the roles that God called me to function in enabled me to more effectively serve the believers and churches that I ministered to.

THE CALL TO GROW IN ADMINISTRATION

With the growing responsibilities of pastoring and counseling came an ever-increasing need to become organized. This was not my forte, and things came to a head when my wife remarked, "How are you going to keep track of your appointments? You've got little slips of paper all over the house!" She suggested, "Why don't you take some courses on organization, so you can figure out what to do?" So, I promptly hired a secretary named Carol to help me get organized at the office.

However, Carol would say, "What are we going to do today?" I suddenly realized that I had to tell her what to do. She said, "Fred, you need to begin to order your events. I think your idea of administration is moving things from your desk to my desk." She added, "Fred, you create a wonderful garden, the problem is it needs extensive weeding."

I began to realize that I had to become more organized. I prayed, and God spoke to me about it. He said, "I speak to you and then you become. It is not by your own effort that you come into what I've called you to." He said to me, "I will make you to become an administrator. It will be by My Spirit and not by your own ingenuity." I then asked Him where to start. I began to write out the night before what was going to happen in my schedule the next day. I started to make little papers to help me know what to do. Then I realized that I needed to do it per week and per month. I also needed to set goals. He further taught me that if I had an agenda when I led meetings, it kept the meeting from straying into discussions that did not accomplishing the goals for the day. As I look back, I realize how the Holy Spirit has made me into an organized person, and the Bezalel anointing is one of the avenues that He has chosen to work through in accomplishing that.

In addition to these things, when I get insights and revelations, I type them out immediately on my computer so that I can refer to them in the future. I find that in many of my conversations and counseling sessions with people, I begin to share something with them, when all of a sudden, I remember a past outline that perfectly fits the present situation. I then go into my database and print it out, and it becomes an answer to their situation. Now, when I am sharing with people, they often jokingly say, "Fred, do you have a sheet on that?" I usually do. I recognize that the Holy Spirit has created a foundation for me to operate as a structured person that I did not have before. I did not have His power that functioned in me in that way. This has become so deeply embedded, that I now think and speak in organized principles, which I never used to be able to do.

THE CALL TO BECOME

Despite God having moved in my life in powerful ways, I still carried an old wound—rejection. There were times when I had felt like a complete failure in life. I was still burdened from years before when no one wanted to be friends with me in youth group. My friends had told me I held them back when they went out with girls. When the boys went out with the girls, I went out to the pond in my neighborhood, and I cried out to God. I told Him that since no one else would listen to me, I would share my heart with Him. I didn't recognize it at the time, but God decided to give me an anointing because I had sought Him out.

All these years later, those old wounds were still an issue, so God led me to an interesting passage in Scripture. He showed me in Exodus 31:1-5 the process by which God chose and equipped Bezalel to carry out His work. In that text, there was a need for a gifted person among the Israelites to bring into reality what God had envisioned. I began to realize that God could totally change a man through anointing him and having His Spirit come upon him.

God said to me, "Bezalel and Hur lived in slavery in Egypt. Bezalel had a slave mentality, and my Spirit anointed Him, took him out of his old cultural setting, and gave Him a new, anointed setting." God also said, "Fred, no matter who you were before, from now on, I will anoint you and tell you what you will become." This promise from God was a significant turning point for me.

Similarly to Bezalel, I had to break out of that old mentality of insignificance. This finally occurred when the Spirit of the Lord came upon me and gave me four things: wisdom, understanding, knowledge and workmanship. These were the same four areas that God deposited in Bezalel. In addition, I discovered that through the anointing of the Lord, Bezalel mentored somebody who had the same background as he did. The implications of this principle were significant in my life. Just as Bezalel was able to effectively mentor once God had anointed him, I too would be able to walk in a new level of mentoring others once that same anointing came to me.

Over the years, I have come to appreciate just how significant this promise of God has been in my life. Whether I do counseling, lead Bible studies, or type out sermons, I now receive wisdom, understanding, and knowledge from the Lord that touches people's lives because of the Bezalel anointing from God. When the anointing comes, you skip eating, you skip sleeping, you give all of your timing to the Holy Spirit, because His timing is not cultural timing. I learned this principle from Dad Ewing's son, Robert, who was a mentor of mine for a number of years. We need God to change who we are to become, and it is important to give Him the room in our lives to execute those changes.

THE CALL TO FATHERHOOD

The call to fatherhood was also more than I bargained for, particularly in relationship to young people who have not been understood or treated properly by their parents. Psalm 68:6 speaks of those who can dwell in families. God brings out the prisoners and the solitary into families. Here God began to speak to me about helping others and having a fathering role in their lives. As a result of this call of God on my wife's life as well as mine, we looked into the Scriptures again to understand what this might entail. First, we understood what Paul was speaking about in 1 Corinthians 4:15, that there were many teachers but few fathers. Paul says, "I became your father through the gospel."

Later, Paul speaks about fathering in 1 Thessalonians 2:10-12 in relation to them as a church. I began to recognize the fathering that the Lord would put into my heart for people. A whole fathering process developed that hinged upon two questions: who should we father and when?

This call to fatherhood in our lives impacted many individuals over the years, some of whom ended up living with us. Joyce Lindstrom was one such person, and she came to us early in her teaching career after having experienced some burnout when she was working in Hastings, MN. She got to know my wife Charlotte, and as a result of Charlotte's desire to include everybody, my wife said, "We need to invite Joyce to live with us and be fathered in our home."

I said, "No, because then I will have to wear pajamas! As of now, I don't have to worry about pajamas, and I don't particularly like them anyhow."

My wife, being a wise woman, asked, "Honey why don't you pray about it?"

Following that conversation, the Lord took me to Isaiah 58, where He describes His true fast, which features taking people into your home. I recognized the principle, but I still didn't want to have to wear pajamas! However, that very day, I sprained my ankle, and had to have my foot up on a pillow. That passage in Isaiah says "…you turn your foot from doing your own pleasure" and it promises that if you take people into your home, "…your recovery will speedily spring forth". So, I acquiesced, my ankle got healed, and that is how Joyce became a part of our family. She has lived with us on-and-off for forty years.

Chapter Four
Starting Churches

Starting the Loring Park Church was quite an experience. I was sitting in Bible class and trying to decide if I should quit school and go share the Lord with people or stay and finish my degree in Social Sciences. I had taken to heart the statistics of how many people die every minute and sensed the eternal destruction awaiting them if no one were to tell them about Christ. As I was experiencing this internal trauma of either being an evangelist or finishing school, I came across a book by David Wilkerson entitled *The Cross and the Switchblade*. As I read that book, I was so touched by the Holy Spirit that I could not put it down. As I read it, I wept for souls.

I must have cried for two hours or more, and I prayed that I would be able to stop crying. My soul gushed out and I could not stop this outpouring of pain and compassion for people who were going to hell. At the end of the reading, when I was finally able to stop crying, I had a vision of a certain building and the word to me was, "Go there and share the gospel."

I was living at home at that time, and I moved into the dorms at Northwestern College. The local area had begun to deteriorate socially, and one morning I saw a dead man floating in the pond and knew that God wanted to do something. As I began walking and praying around that apartment building and came to the front door, I could smell a strong odor. It was like something was dying and smelled really bad. I later found out that a woman who worked as a prostitute had cancer in her sexual organs, and she was the one who smelled. This provoked me to want to share the Lord with people so that they wouldn't find themselves in such situations. I also began to pray and seek God on what to do in the midst of these circumstances.

One day while walking, I met an old business friend who was sharing about the Lord, and he asked if I wanted to pray for the city. I said I was interested, so he rented an office in the Foshay Tower, and we began praying for the city. We met a couple that attended a Baptist church near where I used to live, and they consented to have a Bible study in their apartment. They lived near the building, but not in it, and they were wonderful Christian people. My business friend and I started witnessing and inviting people to Bible study. We met two guys and shared the Lord with them and invited them to come to our first study. When we got to the apartment, we discovered that these two guys had tried to rob the place and were in jail. So we went down to the jail, but the jailer was not going to let us in. As we preached and told him that we were anointed to proclaim the gospel, and that was all the authority that we needed, they got tired of listening to us and let us go in to the two men. One of them was born again in the jail and the other was not interested. We continued hosting the studies, and we were becoming well-known in the area.

One particular incident involved a woman who rejected our preaching. She was attending a Bible study that I was leading. As I was reading in John 4 about the woman at the well who was with a man that was not her husband, this woman ran out terrified, thinking that I had read her mind. She was living with a man at the time. Later, when we were doing door-to-door evangelism, she saw us again and screamed, "Oh no, they have even come here!" Later some of the people we shared with eventually came and attended what we called church.

My business friend was the leading brother and acted as the pastor of the church. He invited a few people from out of town and they came along with some of the people we had shared with. We ended up with about twenty people, including kids and adults. Then I was led by the Lord to go to seminary in Chicago and left the church in those folks' hands to be cared for while I was gone. By Christmas I had returned for vacation and visited the church. During my time in Chicago, I had discovered more of the Holy Spirit and was excited to share it with them. Unfortunately, they did not share the same excitement that I had, and I was dismissed in a kind way. Later, I discovered that the church no longer existed. I prayed and asked the Lord why, and He said that He had removed its candlestick because they rejected the work and ministry of the Holy Spirit.

Revelation 2:5 clearly and definitely gives the basis for repentance, or the candlestick will be removed:

> Remember therefore from whence thou art fallen, and repent, and do the first works; or else I will come unto thee quickly, and will remove thy candlestick out of his place, except thou repent.
>
> (King James Version)

This development clearly brought the fear of the Lord. I realized that God takes these things very seriously and requires us to walk with Him in order to receive His blessing.

While New Testament Church was not the first church that I started, it was the first to incorporate some of the structural model that I had learned about in Waco. Having already given an overview of this church earlier in this book, I would like to share additional details of what God did to bring about its founding.

It was started by a revelation given to me as a pastor of another church at that time. I was pastoring a semi-charismatic, non-denominational (formerly Lutheran) congregation. We were not supposed to raise or clap our hands in time with the music. The limiting aspects were beginning to create some tensions, and I began to seek God. While in this time of praying and seeking the Lord, clear direction came to start a new church.

So, I resigned and began to ask the Holy Spirit to reveal what He wanted to do. The Holy Spirit told me to call up a certain man that I had only interacted with three times in passing, and to tell him that God wanted to start a church in his house. There were to be several other elements for this new church as well. One was that I could not invite anyone, but only tell them about it. The second element was that we would not pass the plate to take offerings, but only have a box where people would give either to the church, the pastor, or to missions. Any money that came in could only be used in the category for which it was designated. In addition, I was told that the Holy Spirit would be the leader and not our tradition, past experiences, or man's ways.

Now with all these elements to consider, and the need to call up this man, I made a list of confirmations that needed to come to pass before I was going to step out on a limb like that. I finally got enough nerve to call, and I said, "God, only if he answers the phone right now will I know this is You and that he will be open to start this church." Then I called. To my amazement, he not only picked up immediately, but informed me that a missionary had come by three weeks before and prophesied that a church would be started in his house! I was so relieved, and we decided to start the very next Sunday. We only knew that two families were committed to coming that first week. Well, it turned out that thirty people showed up and nobody knew who was going to preach or who to write the checks to. I took the lead and spoke on something that came to me, and we decided to call it the New Testament Church. We had all kinds of names like the Last Chance Church, Manna Church, Christian Church, and many more.

Since the church was in its infancy and had not started taking an offering yet, I was without a salary and out of money. On our way to the church at our brother's house, we ran out of gas. I kept praying and telling the Lord we just had to get to the church, and we did. Later, when we went to start the car, it would not start. The brother had some gas, and money was passed along for me to get around. However, even after we poured gas into the gas tank, it still would not start. We eventually had to pour gas directly into the bone-dry carburetor just to get it started. Only later did it dawn on us that we had driven on a completely empty tank. This was going to be a church that operated on faith, and the pastor had to set the example.

After we had been meeting in various locations around the area, we ended up meeting in a very large garage. These church meetings were filled with many miracles. We held our church services in that location both Sunday morning and evening. The presence of the Lord was very heavy, and at various times people were having amazing miracles take place. One miracle occurred when a young woman of the church had a problem with her wisdom teeth not developing properly and the dentist said that they needed to come down for a necessary fit. We prayed for her, and by the power of God, the wisdom tooth came down into its proper place.

When the garage became too small, we met outside and held services both morning and evening during that summer. Minnesota has many mosquitos, so we prayed that we would not be bitten during the service. I claimed Mark 16 as a basis for having authority over the animal kingdom and the insects. What we forgot to do was pray for protection even after the services were over, so that we would not be bitten until we got into the safety of our cars! As soon as we said, "Amen," ending the service, the mosquitos swarmed over us, but they only came after we said, "Amen."

We met at the house in Edina for several months and began to pray and ask for a location to plant this church. I received a word out of Ezekiel 17:1-10 by May Dalberg who did not know what it meant, but it spoke to me of a church plant which would be like a willow tree and spread all over:

> And the word of Jehovah came unto me, saying, Son of man, put forth a riddle, and speak a parable unto the house of Israel; and say, Thus saith the Lord Jehovah: A great eagle with great wings and long pinions, full of feathers, which had divers colors, came unto Lebanon, and took the top of the cedar: he cropped off the topmost of the young twigs thereof, and carried it unto a land of traffic; he set it in a city of merchants. He took also of the seed of the land, and planted it in a fruitful soil; he placed it beside many waters; he set it as a willow-tree. And it grew, and became a spreading vine of low stature, whose branches turned toward him, and the roots thereof were under him: so it became a vine, and brought forth branches, and shot forth sprigs.
>
> There was also another great eagle with great wings and many feathers: and, behold, this vine did bend its roots toward him, and shot forth its branches toward him, from the beds of its plantation, that he might water it. It was planted in a good soil by many waters, that it might bring forth branches, and that it might bear fruit that it might be a goodly vine. Say thou, Thus saith the Lord Jehovah: Shall it prosper? shall he not pull up the roots thereof, and cut off the fruit thereof, that it may wither;

that all its fresh springing leaves may wither? and not by a strong arm or much people can it be raised from the roots thereof. Yea, behold, being planted, shall it prosper? shall it not utterly wither, when the east wind touched it? it shall wither in the beds where it grew.

(American Standard Version)

In a similar vein to this Scripture, I also received a vision of a ring of churches that was going to circle around the entire Twin Cities region. At this point, starting churches was not new because I had received the prototype in the first church. I found that when traveling somewhere on a highway, I would see a sign with a name of a city on it and the Lord would speak to me to start a church in that city.

Often my response would be, "But Lord, I don't know anybody in the city!"

He would respond, "I did not ask you if you knew anybody, but to go start a church in that city."

This process happened over and over until a group of churches was started, and they did circle the Twin Cities just like I saw. Eventually, I formed a network and trained the leaders to work and function in various capacities. The vision had turned into a reality.

A GROWING NETWORK

As this network of churches was growing, both in number and in influence, it encountered an interesting challenge. As the leader and the planter of these churches, I had established congregations from a pastoral vantage point. The focus was primarily on personal ministry and meeting the needs within the individual assembly. This worked well both in leadership and structure as long as there were only a few churches. However, as time went on, not only was the network changing, but God was changing me as well. He began expanding my vision from a primarily pastoral focus to an apostolic one. This was an essential adjustment because I was no longer just overseeing individual congregations, but the network that they were becoming a part of. I could tell that God wanted to accomplish more through us than what we were walking in, but in order to carry out His purposes, we would have to change how we operated as a network.

It is worth noting that the Holy Spirit is not stagnant. I have often found in my walk with Him that He stretches us past our comfort zone and past the ways that we walked in before, even if those ways were God's will for a past season. It can be challenging to exchange the comfort of the familiar for the uncertainty of the unknown. Nevertheless, as we obey in faith and walk in step with His Spirit, He rewards us with His intimacy.

Although I was willing to make the necessary adjustments, not all of the church leaders wanted to adopt these changes. They preferred instead to keep the original, pastorally-focused vision that they were familiar with. Eventually, this led many of the churches in the network to join a new network. This was difficult to watch happen, particularly because over the years, that network stopped growing the way it had in the early days. When we settle for the familiar, we miss God's next opportunity.

THE CHURCH IN CAMBRIDGE

The call to go to Cambridge was a familiar one.

"I want you to start a church in that city."

"But I don't know anybody there!"

"I did not ask you if you knew anybody; I told you to start a church there."

I was invited to share at a forum, and I shared on the ways of God in Psalms 103:7. Later, we started a Bible Study and set a time for the church to begin. The worship leader called just before we were to begin and said, "My sow is sick and has twenty-one piglets, and if she is not healed, I cannot come. If you want me to be able to come, pray for my pig!"

And all the people looked at me and said, "Well, what do you want to do?"

I prayed and said, "God, if You want this church to start, then You have to heal this sow."

A few minutes later he called and said, "She is healed, and I can come to the meeting!" Then we set the time and started the church. Interestingly enough, several hobby farmers ended up attending that church because they heard that sick animals got healed there!

THE CHURCH IN CLOQUET

God spoke to me and said, "Go to Cloquet tonight." Since I was pastoring in Eden Prairie, I went to the people who were leaders in the local church with me to share this word.

Richard Stoner, one of the elders, said, "I don't know what God is doing, but you better get yourself up there!" I agreed that it was the Lord, so I called Eldon Galyen, and asked about having a meeting at somebody's house that evening.

He replied, "Yes, we will arrange it."

I prepared a message that I thought was super-duper and anticipated impacting everyone with my pastoral abilities. When we got there and started the meeting, the pianist could not get into rhythm. Nothing was working—it was dreadful. Then God said, "Are you willing to give up your super-duper message for what I want to do?"

As soon as I gave up my message, the pianist found the right keys and God spoke to me. He said, "This is going to be a body meeting tonight. I am going to have the different members of the body be transported to different places in the Spirit, just like Philip was after being with the Ethiopian eunuch."

So, we prayed, and I said, "I don't know what God is going to do, but we will wait on the Spirit, and He will direct us. Don't be surprised if you end up going somewhere else in the Spirit."

After we prayed and waited a while, I asked for testimonies of where God had sent people. One lady said she went to a mental asylum where a person was under demonic activity in a padded room with secretion on the floor.

She said to the Lord, "What do I do?"

God said: "Pray for her to be healed."

She prayed for the woman and instantly she was healed and returned to her right mind.

I had a similar experience. In the Spirit, I went to a place in Frankfurt, Germany. In a vision-like state, I saw a meeting of a church where the people had just lost their pastor, and they were all crying. I was up in the corner of the room, viewing the meeting below. I asked the Lord what to do, and He said: "Pray that peace will come. I will take away their sorrow and I will give them another pastor."

Two weeks later, I was leading a Bible study back at my church in Eden Prairie, and I felt impressed to tell this story. After this meeting, a young man who was a part of a Lutheran Charismatic group asked me, "Can I see you after the meeting, Fred?" Later he told me, "What you described is exactly what happened in Germany! I was at that meeting—I was there. Everything you said actually took place!"

This church in Cloquet also grew because of a dream. The dream was from a local lawyer who came to me with a hunting vision. He asked me if I interpreted dreams and I told him that I did. In his dream he had been deer hunting and saw a fork in the road. On the right side was an ugly demonic face and on the left side there was a bird with a face on it.

When he asked me what it meant, I told him, "The best I can tell is that you are going down the road of life and you have to choose either the demonic way represented by the ugly face, or the way with the bird on the other side."

The man then said to me, "I'm sorry Fred, I keep staring at your face."

I asked why, and he said, "The face that I saw on the bird was yours, and at the time of the dream I had never met you before."

This was one of the key factors that got the Cloquet church started. The man that had the dream and his colleague were both influential individuals in the area, and their families helped bring more people into the congregation. Today this church is called New Life Community Church in Carlton County, Minnesota.

THE GATE CHURCH

The call of God to St. Paul and South Minneapolis is one that is still continuing. I was at our Sunday night service when I was sensing the anointing of intercession. You cannot predict when the Holy Spirit is going to come upon you. It happened at the church where I was pastoring at the time. I began to weep for the souls of men, and I asked the Lord, "What is this that is coming upon me?"

He said, "It is an intercession for souls in the St. Paul and South Minneapolis area."

The presence of the Lord was upon me for about an hour and a half. Finally, I was able to stop weeping, regain my composure, and started to sense what to do. The first thing I did was to gather some intercessors to fast and pray for those two cities. From this time on, people started to want to get involved with what God was going to do. A dear sister from a previous church named Iris Berg called me and said that we could meet at her home in South Minneapolis. We started to have a Bible study and teaching every Friday night. From those training and teaching meetings, several young people were established in the Lord and a church resulted. It was called Uptown Fellowship, which is now called The Gate, located in St. Louis Park, Minnesota.

I met a man who was an evangelist and was working in Christiansted, U.S. Virgin Islands. He was impressed with the concept of a New Testament type of church rather than a mainline denominational type of church structure. After we had talked for a while, he invited me to come down and help him start a New Testament church in Christiansted. We planned our trip when it was the least expensive time of the year to go.

As we went down to Florida, it seemed like a normal flight. All was good as we took our flight pattern up, but as soon as we left Florida, I said to my wife, "We are entering into another demonic sphere."

Here is where a spiritual sense needs to come into play because my wife Charlotte did not notice anything at all. As I prayed, God gave me a vision of the demonic sphere and strategy that I was about to enter into. I asked the Lord how to deal with this demonic realm. He said, this one will only be overcome by three days of fasting and drinking only water. When we arrived, the brother and his wife wanted to take us out to dinner right on the waterfront, but I responded that I would take a rain check because of the fast for starting the church.

I asked the Lord what His strategy was in relation to this demonic realm. I was told that this demonic entity had been there for years and that it was connected to slavery from when the Dutch first started the sugar plantations. I saw this circle of demonic beings that had a main spirit-being over them. God said they had never been dealt with because people had just dealt with the outer rings and never reached the main one that was the leader.

When I got to our friend's home, I went into the bedroom assigned to us, and that demonic spirit pressed me down until I collapsed on the bed. As I was passing out from the pressure, I prayed that God would call upon the intercessors to help me. The next thing I knew, I woke up from that ordeal unable to move. I tried to get up, but nothing would move, and so I said, "In the name of Jesus, I can lift my head." Under the pressure, I was able to move my head. Then I tried to move my arm, and it would not move no matter how hard I tried. Again, I declared, "In the name of Jesus, I can move my arm."

So, this process went on for every part of my body. It took three days to overcome this demonic power that controlled the island. After the first day, I could begin to move around and function with the family we were staying with. Toward the end of the three days, I had a vision of the demonic power sliding off to one side. After the time was finished, we went to dinner and I said, "Now we can begin the church."

I made several trips down to help the church, and I took other brothers along for training and for allowing their gifts to function in a new setting. My ministry in St. Croix eventually ended when a local Cruzan doctor spread a rumor about me that I was a racist. My friend and pastor said, "I would love to have you come back, but the Cruzan people will not accept you any longer." While this was obviously a disappointing way for my time there to end, I am still grateful to the Lord for allowing me to help start that church. The lessons that I learned, and the power of God that I witnessed left a lasting impression on me.

One particular time comes to mind when a service lasted all morning and into the afternoon. The presence of the Lord was extraordinarily strong that day, so it was determined to have three lines for people to get ministered to. I was given the healing line, another brother who came along with me was given the baptism of the Holy Spirit line, and the pastor the line of those to receive Christ. I noticed that my line never seemed to get any shorter. I eventually realized that once those in the other lines were finished, they would come and get into my line. That day a lady came with a spinal problem, and she was only able to walk with great difficulty. She was miraculously healed and came back that night with her testimony. All afternoon she ran up and down the stairs in their house to show people what God had done for her!

Chapter Five
How to Get Rid of that Demon

When I attended Northwestern College in Minneapolis, before they moved to Roseville, I heard stories from our Bible professor that people could be set free from demons. Dr. Hartel would share and make the New Testament Survey come alive with his stories. On the very evening following one such morning class, as I was sleeping, I felt something come into my bedroom and the presence of it was smothering. But I remembered to use the name of Jesus, and it slowly began to leave the room. While this was perhaps my first real awareness of a demonic spirit on a personal level, it would be some time before I recognized demons manifesting through other people.

This all changed when I lived in Chicago. While in seminary, I heard stories about a woman who was demonized walking in the street near Grace Tabernacle, which was located on Grace Street. Well, I went down to find out what these people were talking about, only to find a seemingly old woman with several teeth missing. She was also wearing an old heavy coat which was too big for her. However, the oddest part was that she stood in the middle of the street, growling like a dog. When I saw that, I turned my car around in the middle of the road and went back to seminary. I knew this was out of my league.

Later, during my time as a youth pastor at Edgewater Covenant, I met a Baptist youth minister named Jim. He was working in the same area and among the same gang members as I was. I found out that he was a draftee for the Chicago Bears and had been led to the Lord by Y.A. Tittle, a leading quarterback at that time. After getting to know him better, he told me he had a problem and asked if I could help him. When he picked up kids and would haul them around, they would get out of the little V.W. Beetle, and the car door would shut by itself without anyone touching it. Jim was hoping we could get the demon—or whatever it was—to stop interfering with his ministry and cause this spiritual thing that was happening to stop. So, I got into the car, and we prayed and broke the demon that was involved, and it then stopped opening and shutting the door.

With this success behind us, I was asked for another favor. Jim told me that his brother, who was involved in the crime syndicate in Chicago, had a problem. He said, "When my brother was sitting at dinner last night, he just fell forward into the mashed potatoes, sound asleep." I went over to their apartment for dinner, and as we prayed, his brother got delivered from a number of demonic activities that were bothering him.

My next encounter with the demonic came when I was picking out an apartment in the Edgewater area of Chicago. I was planning to get married, so Charlotte and I looked at this potential future home together. While we were there, we felt this strange feeling of evil, but I rented the apartment anyway. Later I had my future brother-in-law Scott and friend Jim see this apartment, and we again felt something evil in the place. We all agreed it was demonic, and because it was my apartment, it was my responsibility to go first and get this thing out of there. Well, when we went to the closet the evil got stronger, so we knew it was located there. The bedroom with the closet lead toward the

44

kitchen. We wanted to make sure that the spirit could find its way out, so we even propped the back door open with a chair. The others decided that it was my turn to lead, so I opened my Bible and stuck it into the closet to make the evil to come out. It did. The hair on the back of our necks stood straight up. We decided to all hold hands. As that spirit left the closet, it pushed Scott, Jim, and me out of the way and exited the apartment through the back door.

RELEASING THE CAPTIVES

In our early ministry time in Minneapolis, we started a coffee house on Lake Street with a surprise on the very first night. When the time came to open, all the lights on that side of the street went dark. The lights did not come back on until right at closing time. We came in the next week and prayer walked the street and felt that a witch's coven was causing the problems. After we took authority in the Spirit and broke the power of the enemy, we had no more issues with the lights going on and off.

That week we had two women come into the coffee house, and through the ministry, they gave their lives to the Lord. It turned out that they were both prostitutes for the crime machine in the area and were a part of a local witchcraft coven as well. One of the women got her life cleaned up and then went back to Rockford, Illinois and started over in a local church. One year later, I got a letter from her thanking me for the help we gave and sharing how she got back into church and was making a change in her life. The other woman came to our local church and was being counseled and helped in her new Christian life. Several of the vices that had taken hold of her were broken, and her little daughter began to get involved in our church.

A few months later, another young woman, whom we will call Mary, came to us. She was also a witch and went to the University of Minnesota caves to commune with the spirits there. She also wanted to give her life to the Lord but had no place to live. So, the director of the coffee house called us up and decided to bring her to our house to get help. Well, this was quite an undertaking because she kept hearing voices telling her to go down to our basement. We had prayers for her that sometimes lasted all day and all night. There were teams that would take turns in praying and also trying to keep her from pulling her hair out by the roots. One particular session lasted almost around the clock, and eventually she came out of a catatonic state and seemed to be better. She had several needs, so Charlotte went and bought her some clothes and tried to help her with personal hygiene.

Another story of God's amazing power is when I was a part of a Bible study meeting in the Basler's home and a woman who had two Grand Mal Seizures a day came for prayer. She was prayed for, and she was set free from a spirit that was attacking her. My friends, Ed and Bruce, were involved in getting a church started as a result of that woman's healing or deliverance, whichever people want to call it. The Scripture in Acts 10:38 clearly declares that Jesus Christ heals all those oppressed by the devil. This woman was oppressed by the devil, and she was set free. The funny thing was that the brothers never bothered to tell me that she was completely free because they said, "We did not think you needed to know that because you experience it all the time!"

While pastoring a church called Living New Covenant Church, we had a family attend that was a blended family unit. I was involved in family counseling regarding the father and his relationship to the son of the wife. The young man was about twelve years old and was losing a pound of weight a week. His mother had been feeding him every kind of malt possible in an unsuccessful effort to make him to gain weight. One Sunday morning after church, the mother asked if we could please pray for her son. As we began to pray, I saw a curse of death with a death spirit over him.

The Lord revealed to me that someone had to get in-between the boy and the spirit in order for this young man to live. I took the challenge and stood between the boy and the death spirit and commanded the curse to be broken because of Christ's work on the cross. This process took a good half hour or more, and with intense prayer, the spirit began to leave the young man. At first it would not move, but after declaring what the Word of God says, it withdrew from the boy. It took one last challenge, but then turned and left the young man. The report came back a few weeks later that from that day forward, the youth began to gain weight and was saved from the threat of death.

Chapter Six
Bringing God's Kingdom to the Business World

After leaving Chicago, my wife and I came back to Minnesota and got involved in the local community. During this time, I began working for Bob, a man who ran a business called Creative Associates. I discovered that I was hired to hear from the Lord and to discern which business clients would be paying clients and which ones would not be. Bob and I would pray together and then I would go interview people for a magazine about the business. In this capacity, I traveled around the country as an interviewer, engaging with individuals from various companies. On many of the trips I would meet people and share the Lord with them.

I remember a particular time when I went to Durango, Colorado, where you fly in between the mountain peaks. Upon arrival, I had a limo driver take me from the airport to my business interview. I finished my interview and got the same limo driver again on the way back. This time we were alone, so I shared Christ with him, and he received the Lord that day.

It was during this time that our regular secretary for the office went on vacation, and a "Kelly Girl" came to take her place for two weeks. I got to know her and shared the Lord with her. Several years later, I went to visit a church elder, and he had his neighbor over. As I walked in, I said to the neighbor, "Don't I know you?"

She said, "Yes Fred, you were the one who led me to Christ when I was a temporary worker in your office." God has His ways to let us know how wondrously He works.

As I was growing in business and witnessing, I was given a task to engage in study concerning the business enterprise and the Kingdom of God. The study developed into a rather large and concentrated vision of what business should be like. One of the things that came out of this study was what I called the "Joseph Ministry." Although I didn't realize it at the time, other people were receiving a similar message from the Lord. A key element in this ministry is the anointing that Joseph received. This anointing releases God's favor on a person whom God has destined to be involved in His Kingdom work. Just as in Joseph's life, God is able to raise up unlikely individuals out of dark places and elevate them to tremendous positions through His favor and equipping. As I got involved in other business enterprises along with pastoring, it became quite an adventure becoming a "Joseph person."

Several years later, I left that company because God put me out of business for a season and said, "Now you cannot make any more money at your job. I am going to make you go into the ministry."

EAST COAST ADVENTURES

Three years following this transition, God spoke to me to go and see Bob again. I had a sense that I was to go to New York and do ministry there, but I had no money to travel to New York. While sitting in Bob's office, he asked, "Fred, do you want to go to New York?"

I said, "Yes, as a matter of fact, I do!"

"OK. Meet me at the airport tomorrow morning, and we will travel together. We will see what the Lord puts into our hands."

The next morning, I was at the airport to meet Bob. He gave me my ticket and we boarded the plane. During the flight I glanced at the ticket, and to my great surprise, we were flying to Washington, D.C., not New York. I thought, *how is this going to work?* Once we landed, we met some businessmen who asked us where we were staying and what hotel they could take us to. Bob informed them that we had left in such a hurry that we still needed to get a hotel. One of the businessmen had connections in the area and said that he could get us into Washington, D.C.'s Mayflower Hotel. My mind started racing because I did not have any money—I was only going along with Bob! I had to think very quickly because it was time to pay for the room. I wrote the man a check, but I knew we did not have that amount of money in that checkbook. As I left for my room, Bob said, "If you want to go to New York, be downstairs at 5:00 AM in the morning and you can ride with me."

I went to my room and began to pray and ask God for the money to pay for the room. I also called my wife and told her what I had done. Her response has always been supportive, and her willingness to trust God never ceases to amaze me. God was faithful to us and the next morning fifty dollars in cash was in our mailbox. My wife was then able to deposit the money and the check that I wrote did not bounce.

Well, I was downstairs at 5:00 AM and got into the car with Bob and his associate and off to New York we went.

When we got to downtown New York, Bob suddenly said, "Here, I will drop you off right here."

As I stepped out of the car, it was noon on Wall Street. I got out and thought, *what do I do now?* It came to me that I had a phone number of a man named John from Minneapolis who had family in New York, and I called him. When he asked me where I was staying, I told him that I just arrived, and he invited me to come and stay at his sister's apartment for the night.

I stayed with them for a few days. It ended up that while I was there, I started a little church in Spanish Harlem. It was there that some of his friends knew a student who needed deliverance from witchcraft. I told them I would try to help them with their friend who attended Union Seminary. It was quite a deliverance and God was faithful to us and to the young student. The friends were also amazed and grateful for what had happened. After the deliverance and dinner with the friends of the student, a brother told me that he had a dream about me the night before. "I saw a garbage truck, and the driver was you! The sign on the truck read, 'This is God's garbage man.'"

John's sister was going up to New Canaan, Connecticut by train. She asked me if I wanted to come along because she thought it would be a place to minister. We did end up ministering, and the meeting went too long to make the train back to New York, so we all stayed in a lady's house that night.

She said to her friend, Audrey Buck, "I cannot have a man sleep in my house because my husband would go crazy!"

So, Audrey invited me to her house to stay. When we arrived, her husband was furious.

He said, "I sent you out for cleaning supplies and you come back with a preacher!"

Then he turned to me and asked, "Do you know how to work? Here, help me clean up my basement and all this soot. Find a broom and get to work."

I ended up helping to clean up their basement and we became friends. Audrey shared that God had been speaking to her about their daughter Melanie in Atlanta who was not following the Lord. She asked, "If I gave you the money to go see her, would you do it?" I said I would if God told me to.

After returning home from that trip, as I was having my devotions, God clearly spoke to me. He said, "Tomorrow I want you to go to

Atlanta, Georgia and share the gospel with Audrey's daughter." The next morning, I asked Charlotte to take me to the airport, and I got a ticket to Atlanta. Upon arriving, I only had Melanie's phone number and tried to find a hotel room. But there was none to be found, so I waited in the prayer chapel at the airport.

I suddenly remembered the name of a visiting preacher from Georgia who had previously shared at my church, so I called him. He was mad and rebuked me for not planning ahead, but because I had previously had him at my church, he consented to help me. I got a room that night and called Melanie and let her know that I wanted to see her.

Her response was "Did my mother send you?"

I said, "Yes, that was how I got your phone number."

She then plainly informed me, "I don't like preachers. I will meet you for lunch but that is all."

We met for lunch, and she said, "I will give you a ride to my office and from there you can get a limo to the airport."

Now, all the money I had was twenty dollars, just enough to get to the airport. While at lunch I had tried to share Christ, but she would have none of it. I was sitting in her office, and she was very angry with me, so I thought, *well, one last try.*

I said to her, "You are a chain smoker. If Jesus gave you peace, would you accept Him?"

Her answer was, "OK, OK, just get it over with and get out of here."

So, I went over and prayed for her and the peace that came over her was amazing. She almost fell off the chair. It was my time to leave for the limo and I walked out the door.

When she came home that day, her husband was sitting in the bathroom window, thinking he was a bird. She said, "Come down, honey! You are not a bird. A crazy pastor that my mother sent told me to accept Jesus!"

They both ended up giving their lives to the Lord. Eventually, they worked at an Episcopalian church that was moving powerfully in the Holy Spirit and had an outreach that touched Atlanta. Over the years, they led countless people to Christ.

Of course, I did not know all of that at the time. On the flight home I was complaining to the Lord about how difficult that trip had been.

I asked, "God, why did You not simply send someone to walk across Peach Tree Street to tell that woman about Jesus?"

The Lord spoke to me and said, "I came all the way from heaven to earth to die on a cross for you. Is Atlanta, Georgia too far for you to go for Me?"

I cried the whole way home. I have never forgotten that word and decided from that day forward that no distance is too far to go for Jesus.

Chapter Seven
I'm Healed! How Did You Do That?

Dr. Fred Smith, the British professor who challenged me to share the gospel, was a very important person to me in my beginning years. It turned out that he had cancer, and I did not really understand the ramifications that went along with that. Being so involved with this man, I took on his healing in a very personal way. I prayed for him and believed in what I was doing, but he ended up dying. I felt devastated and was concerned that if I prayed for any more people, that they too would die. Therefore, I did not pray for anyone for almost two years after that instance.

While I was a youth pastor at Edgewater Covenant Church in Chicago, I was visiting with a family in their home, and they made a request for healing. The family was made up of a married couple and their relative from Armenia, named Gayle. After I prayed for and ministered to the family, Gayle was so grateful that she promised to pray for me three times a day from then on. She kept that promise, and for years I was the recipient of her heavenly petitions. I did not know how to act or how to receive such depths of gratitude. This was a much-needed encouragement to me in praying for others to be healed. Gayle showed me what it meant to be fervent in the Spirit, and her resolve in the Lord became a signpost that led me deeper into the supernatural.

This victorious episode of prayer for healing took me back many years to when I was in grade school. At that time, whenever I came home from school, I had to check if my mother was in an insulin shock and be ready to give her an insulin shot. Over the years she had to take her insulin and it began to affect her body and the circulation in her lower extremities. On one of these trips home, my mother asked if I would pray for her right leg because it was beginning to turn brown from a lack of circulation. Unless something was to change, it would result in an amputation of her leg. We began to pray, and the power of God was present. The leg started to change color and her circulation started happening right there! Years later she showed me her right leg and contrasted it to the left one. The leg that was healed permanently had better color than the other one.

ANOINTING IN THE PHILIPPINES

One day years later, the Lord spoke to me and said, "Your friend is lonely, go visit him." That brother's name was Bobby Martz, and he lived and ministered in the Philippines. It ended up being quite a trip, and took thirty-four hours in travel time by plane, boat, bus, and car. After being there awhile, Bobby asked me to speak one night. Following the message, we discovered that so many people needed healing from deafness that he asked them to form two lines. He took one line and told me to take the other. The results were amazing! In both lines many people were healed from deafness that night. My brother Bobby has a gift of faith for healing and sees many miracles in his ministry. As I submitted to his leadership at that meeting, the anointing that he operated in was able to function through me. After returning home, I was asked to hold special healing meetings in some of the churches that I was affiliated with because of the amazing things that God did on that trip.

One particular meeting was held in Cloquet, Minnesota. At that meeting the power of the Holy Spirit came down for about ninety seconds and people were healed and set free. Following that move of the Spirit, I prayed a general prayer and then asked if anyone had received a healing. Cervical cancer, ovarian cancer, and several other sicknesses were totally eradicated in people's bodies. A certain man exclaimed that his pain was gone! His condition was from a work-related accident, and he consequently had an operation that fused the discs in his back. The backpain had become so severe that it took him twenty minutes to get out of bed every morning. I asked him to testify, but he said that he needed to wait until after the following morning, so he would know for sure if the pain was really gone. The next night he came to the service and shared that in the morning he had feared the pain would still be there, but it was completely gone.

Afterwards his question was, "What do I do now?" He had been on complete disability, and I told him it was time to go back to work. I was not sure whether he would follow through or whether he had gotten used to retirement.

One of the keys to those tremendous meetings came from entering into a new place with God. For lack of a better term, it was like entering into a certain anointed vein in the Spirit. Once I was in it, powerful prophetic words, healings, miracles, breakthroughs in spiritual warfare, and other spiritual experiences would take place.

While these encounters with God's power were riveting, there was another, more difficult side to those experiences as well. After some of these healing meetings would end, I struggled in being able to communicate with people. To my surprise, I couldn't quite shift back out of that spiritual vein once I had entered into it. I could hear what people were trying to say to me, but I couldn't concentrate or communicate. It was as though we were operating on different frequencies, as distinct as AM and FM radios.

On one of these occasions, I left the people I was with and went looking for a secure, out-of-the-way place to be alone. I found a dark room with a chair in the corner and just sat there. It took a while for the anointing to lift, but as it did, I felt like I was coming back down into the realm that other people were operating out of. Once I was fully functional again, I could rejoin and interact with others. However, what lingered was a strong desire to experience that anointing all over again.

This occurrence gave me perspective on how certain Christian leaders and famous evangelists went from having thriving ministries to losing everything. They had experienced the exhilarating effects of the anointing, but once it lifted, they tried to recreate the same experience using fleshly avenues like drugs and alcohol. The issue was that they didn't have accountability. They allowed the praise of others to gradually convince them that they were invincible. Never allow the acclaim that comes from moving in the anointing change your identity. Operating in the power of God needs to be coupled with wisdom in order to have a lasting impact.

AN APPEAL FROM GERMANY

Over the years, God allowed me to plant churches in many parts of the world, and one of those places was Germany. Charlotte and I got to know a German woman there, and we became spiritual parents to her. We would meet with her during our visits and talk on the phone when we were back in the U.S. One day this woman called me feeling very discouraged. She was struggling to feel loved by God because she was unable to get pregnant. She said, "Fred, whenever you come and minister in-person, God moves powerfully, and miracles happen.

Would you fly to Germany to pray for me to have a baby?" I told her that I would ask God about it.

When I took this situation to prayer, I said, "God, I care about this woman, but do You want me to fly all the way across the ocean just so that she can feel loved by You?"

He said, "Yes, I do. Remember the vow that you made to Me after your trip to Atlanta, Georgia. You said that no distance was too far to go for Me."

I was deeply touched by God's heart of compassion for this woman. He wanted so much for her to know His love. So, I flew to Germany and prayed for her in-person, as she had requested. Within a couple of weeks of my return home, she contacted us. You already know the end of the story—we serve an amazing God! He heard her heart; she was pregnant.

Chapter Eight
Stalking the Demon World for the Kingdom of God

The book of Nehemiah outlines the cardinal, unchanging strategies that the enemy uses to divert people from God's purposes. This old, yet present plan has four basic steps or stratagems in it. The first is simply ridicule, the second is physical force, the third is fear, and the fourth is character assassination. These steps were all employed against the Jews in Nehemiah's time as they were trying to obey God and rebuild Jerusalem. Our enemy tries to find which of these tactics will be most effective against a person and then keeps using them until the believer finally makes him stop.

AN EARLY CHALLENGE

One of my first prayer assignments as a new pastor was to help a person who was going through a difficult challenge to his sexuality. The young man had homosexual feelings, knew that he didn't want them, and desired to be biblical in his sex life. I took the opportunity to pray with and for him. While doing that, I encountered the demonic spirit that was harassing him, and we took spiritual authority over that spirit. The young man received a measure of immediate relief from the pressure to join the homosexual lifestyle.

That was on a Sunday afternoon. By Monday morning, I was feeling quite sick and was lying in bed. We had three young children at the time and my wife thought I was enjoying being sick a little too much. In fact, many of the women in my wife's prayer circle were comparing notes about how *helpless* their husbands acted when they "got sick". Unfortunately for me, my condition was genuinely miserable.

After the sickness lingered on and on, I finally got tired of being sick and asked the Lord what was going on. It was then that I began to learn about the shield of faith found in Ephesians 6:11. After I restored my shield and exercised my faith, the sickness left me.

Many lessons were learned from that experience. I understood that when we engage in spiritual warfare, the enemy tries to retaliate. I may have been prepared for the initial battle that led to the young man's release, but I was unprepared for the pushback that came as a consequence. Utilizing the shield of faith has since become a mainstay for me in doing ministry. There are many other ways to protect yourself from the enemy's retaliation, including praying through Psalm 91. The important thing is to be prepared when you pray for others and not to be ignorant of the enemy's schemes (2 Corinthians 2:11, Ephesians 6:11).

Another key that I gleaned from that experience was learning the principle of spirit-transfer. In a given battle or situation, demonic spirits rise to fight the highest spiritual authority involved in that arena. When I had prayed for that young man, the demonic sprit that was afflicting him recognized that I was operating in a greater level of spiritual authority than the young man was. As a consequence, that spirit climbed the spiritual authority ladder and went from attacking him to attacking me!

Incidentally, this principle works both ways. I often find that when I am dealing with a number of demonic spirits over a person, I ask God which one is the leader or the "strong man" in the group. As is the case in gang wars, once the gang leader is removed, the rest of the gang scatters.

On the positive side, once you know how demonic realms function in spiritual warfare, you can prepare to counter their strategies. In fact, sometimes the way in which spirits transfer up the chain of command can be to our advantage. For example, this allows a godly leader who operates in spiritual authority to provide a covering to other Christians. As these Christians submit to the covering of that leader, the demonic spirits that would otherwise attack them have to go deal with the leader that they are under. This forms a kind of spiritual umbrella that keeps those under it from getting rained on. Of course, this also requires the leader to be mature in spiritual authority because he or she will have to deal with the demons that come from those that submit under that umbrella.

A BATTLE FROM GERMANY

I had a friend who was on a ministry trip through Europe that finished up in Germany. The night before his departure, a demonic prince from the city where he was ministering visited him in his room. My friend made a snide remark to this demonic realm and the spirit prince began a spiritual attack against him. Well, this spirit followed him back home, making him sick and making life difficult in other ways as well. So, my friend called me, and we prayed together.

As I was in the spirit and praying, I saw a dot that was way out in the atmosphere, and it was coming closer. It got bigger and bigger until it finally dropped down through the ceiling into the living room where

I was praying! This demonic prince was so big that he filled the whole room. As he brought his hand over me, his thumb was on my head and his little finger on my foot, and I was about to get crunched. As I was crying out to God, the Scripture that came to mind was "By the power of His might" from Ephesians 6. When I spoke these words out loud, the demonic prince stopped in his tracks. I thought to myself, *if it worked once, it might work again*. I repeated the phrase and that prince started backing up. When I said it a third time, he left, and the battle was over.

After that encounter, I recognized the need to study the sixth chapter of Ephesians in greater depth. The key to unpacking that phrase in Ephesians 6:10 was found in Ephesians 1:19-23. Here I discovered that the Father operated in that mighty power to raise Jesus from the dead, and He allows this same power to operate towards believers. I concluded that the maturity level of our relationship with Christ is the degree that we can operate in authority over the enemy.

STRATEGIC STALKING

We can even stalk the enemy when the person that has a demonic situation thinks that it is only their personality and not a demon. When I encounter this type of situation, I proceed to antagonize the demonic identity so that it will expose itself, allowing the person to realize that the behavior is not them.

A good illustration of this principle occurred with a man who attended a church that I was leading. He was an ex-military man and was very successful in selling insurance door-to-door because he intimidated people until they would buy the insurance. However, this behavior occurred not only in door-to-door sales, but in his family and in the church. I told this man what the situation was, but he did not initially believe it.

He defiantly said, "Since my wife and my pastor both say it is true, I have to believe it."

We began speaking about the Blood of Jesus and immediately he had a reaction, making it clear that this was not him. Then he believed, and we were able to get him delivered from this demonic problem. The issues all went back to his dad's abuse of his mother, and when he stood up to his dad, the spirit left his dad and attached to him.

A similar situation occurs when a Christian has a spirit of rejection and does not realize it. In this case, whoever is helping me begins to tell the person all the good things we know about them. We begin to express how the Lord loves them and how His love will set the captive free until the spirit begins to manifest itself. The manifestations can include suddenly feeling sick, having to go to the bathroom, or suddenly getting a headache. Another manifestation is thinking, *I have to go home right now, and I cannot continue this meeting anymore.* These are all manifestations of avoidance.

TRIALS IN THAILAND

Sixteen years ago, I encountered the Red Dragon on a trip to Southeast Asia. My wife had an intercessory team going to Southeast Asia and wanted me to come along because a husband of one of the other intercessors was coming. We had several prayer times in preparation for this trip. One of the times was at our home and I had a vision of a demonic Spirit that was red in color. I asked God what this was all about and what instructions He had for us. The answer was quite simple.

"There are three parts to the trip: the first is preparation, the second is getting there and the third is getting home." Little did I know how true that word was going to be. Due to an earlier car accident, my knee had been hurt, and it was still sore. When we arrived at the airport in Thailand, my knee was really beginning to hurt.

I still preached in Malaysia and afterwards came back to Thailand, but by then I could not walk. I ended up in several hospitals and saw many doctors, but it was unclear just what was wrong. Finally, I ended up in a good hospital in Bangkok. My stay lasted five weeks and I almost died there. I encountered demonic manifestations, unnatural sexual dreams, culture shock, loneliness, and depression.

The physical battle that I was experiencing was a reflection of a larger, spiritual conflict that I found myself in. It was difficult overcoming the demonic realms in Thailand, and I was initially unsure of the reason why. Eventually the Lord revealed that the demonic realms in Thailand were subservient to a larger enemy power called the Red Dragon. This is the demonic realm that rules over China, and it rather reminded me of the dragon mentioned in the Book of Revelation. It was challenging to face such a battle in a foreign country, particularly because the people with me did not know how to deal with it. They eventually backed away and let the issue go. Unfortunately for me, I was the target of the enemy's attack, so I couldn't do the same.

After several weeks, I was finally released from the hospital and got back to the U.S., but I still had to go to Mayo Clinic in Rochester, Minnesota. Aside from the warfare, something else was transpiring in the spirit realm. In 2 Corinthians 1:8-11 we read about Paul's experiences in Asia and that the believers were praying for him. It was the grace of God and the prayers of these people that saved Paul's life. It was clear that my experience was just like what Paul had gone through. I thanked all the people that I knew had prayed for me when I returned home and was well enough to visit the churches.

God also used the afflictions that Paul suffered as a way to reveal His comfort to him. In the same chapter in 2 Corinthians, Paul suddenly found himself equipped to minister God's comfort to others in the same way in which he had been comforted. In the months following this ordeal in Thailand, I encountered many individuals whom God rescued through the lessons that He had taught me in this process. Several people who were unable to share their struggles with anyone suddenly felt like they could share them with me, even without knowing what I had recently gone through. God is masterful at turning the most difficult situations into glorious victories!

Chapter Nine
Living in Two Worlds Simultaneously

A further extension into the supernatural in my life came in a very unusual way. I had an appointment for lunch with a Christian businessman at a downtown Minneapolis restaurant and I arrived a little bit early. What unfolded in front of me was surprising. As I was waiting, I suddenly saw two worlds superimposed on each other. I changed from being just a businessman in the rush and bustle of the lunch break, to suddenly seeing all the people in the restaurant with demonic attachments on them!

Every demonic activity that was operating in their lives had a vapor attached to them in that particular part of their body. At first, I thought I was having a dirty mind, but I later realized there was no lust of any kind attached to what I saw or felt. I prayed and asked the Lord what was happening, and He shared with me that these two worlds were operating all the time and I was just now seeing them for what they really were! Little did I know that this was the beginning of a different lifestyle for me and was going to affect me the rest of my life.

Before you, the reader, get all excited about this kind of lifestyle, let me tell you that it also has some very lonely moments that go along with it. Just think—once you are in this position, who can you talk to about the things that you see? Those demons are attached to someone and besides that, who really wants to know? Once people begin to realize that you see into them and various things about them, they start to avoid you and treat you like you have the plague or something. One day I went to church and people were staying as far away from me as possible. I began to feel rejected and even thought I had better check my deodorant.

Another interesting thing that began to happen at various times was that the Holy Spirit would come upon me, regardless of where I was. Many times, a prophetic word would come suddenly—even at a dinner meal or when I was out to lunch with someone. I have a close friend that I go to lunch with quite often, and he says that sometimes I go into the heavenlies while we are sharing together.

SEEING WHAT HE SEES

Learning to operate with God like this occurred in stages. While ministering in Chicago, I asked God for a vision for the city. I was beginning to join some church friends on Saturday mornings who were praying for the vision that God had for us. After praying for several weeks, the Lord taught me the ways to receive vision. He told me that in order to have His vision I had to be willing to see what He saw. Next, I had to be willing to hear what He heard. Finally, I had to be willing to feel what He felt.

The vision started out by Him revealing lonely people to me and allowing me to really see them. Then the scene changed, and His focus was on people being abused. Finally, He highlighted abortion and all the murdered babies in the city. He actually took me to each of these places in the vision so that I could see, hear, and feel what He did. It was overwhelming to me. I later found the Scripture in Exodus 3 where God comes down to Moses because He had heard, seen and felt the suffering of the Israelites and determined to send someone to help lead them out of Egypt. This experience, while challenging, opened up a new way of engaging with God's heart and purposes for people.

INTERCESSION TOUCHING TWO WORLDS

I was praying at our Saturday night intercession group when the Lord unexpectedly instructed us to prepare to meet people's needs anywhere in the world. The Lord said that He was going to take me to another city where a young person was in need. I found myself in a spiritual state where I entered a room where a young girl, about twelve years old, was dead and her parents were crying about their daughter. When I entered the room above them, I asked God what I was supposed to do.

He said, "Raise her from the dead." So, I did, and she got up and her parents were hugging her. Then I came back to the prayer meeting. Some of the other people had similar experiences that night.

One particular time that made an impression on me, took place at a Saturday night intercession meeting at my house. We knew that two needs were a part of the agenda for that prayer time. One was that my daughter needed ten thousand dollars for her mission trip to France. The other was a businessman who needed forty thousand dollars that week. In our time of praying in tongues we often hear what the instructions for the night will be. This time I heard, "You are going to go into the heavenlies where you have been seated in Christ Jesus according to the Scriptures."

At the time I was sitting in a big chair, and I could literally feel the liftoff in such a way that I grabbed the sides of the chair, to hold on! I was taken up into the spirit realm to the place where the demonic spirits that control money over cities are located. I saw the one over Chicago, and another one over Atlanta. I was given clear instructions

71

on what to say, and what not to say, to these demonic powers. I saw other ruling spirits as well, but I was told not to speak to or command them, because without protection, they could kill me. So, we did what we were told to do, and the result was that on the following Sunday afternoon, my daughter was promised the ten thousand dollars. Later that week the businessman also received a loan for the money he needed.

A MEMORABLE ROAD TRIP

I was traveling on Hwy. 90 from Minneapolis to Illinois. I had been invited to speak at a house church in McHenry, Illinois. I was traveling with three other men in a Volvo station wagon, which was old enough that when you drove downhill, the rubber binder would get tight, and then going uphill, it would unwind.

I stopped in Madison, WI. to call the man who invited me, telling him, "I'm sorry, but I don't think we can get there on time."

He said, "We have already announced that a special speaker will be sharing—and it's you! Let's pray that you can still make it on time."

So, we had to keep going. I was driving, two guys were sleeping in the back seat, and the other was in the passenger's seat. We were behind a truck, and it was raining really heavily, so I prayed, "Lord, if we are to get there on time, you have to do something real quick!" Then, all of the sudden, I was driving up a hill in bright sunlight into a city.

The passenger said, "Where are we?"

I said, "If I am not mistaken, we are in McHenry, Illinois."

I had been there before, so we drove to the house meeting. Upon arrival, we were one minute early! We later figured out that we had traveled the hour-and-forty-five-minute stretch from Madison to McHenry (93 miles) in one minute. I don't remember what I spoke on that evening, but I have never forgotten the way I arrived!

Chapter Ten
Leaving the Bleachers and Returning to the Game!

As believers, we all face difficulties in our lives. A chief obstacle arises when we find ourselves at a crossroads and need to hear the voice of the Lord clearly. This occurred in my own life when I was living in the Chicago area and was just learning about hearing from God. I so much wanted to listen to and know His voice and desired to do His will.

During this time period, I was looking for a place to live and wanted the Lord to direct me. I said, "Lord, I will drive wherever you tell me to go." Well, at this time of wanting to be open, I felt and saw a bright light come into my car. I wanted to obey and find out where God wanted me to go. I opened up my mind to receive directions and was told what street to drive to, and sure enough, there was a house for sale.

So, my wife and I would regularly drive by this place, and I even told people this was to be our house. This lasted until one day we drove by and saw a sold sign on the front of the house. We were devastated in our faith and in hearing the voice of God. Later we found a house, but it was in Minnesota, not in Illinois. What a lesson concerning hearing voices and looking for lights to guide us! Later the passage where we have the mind of Christ became a very real help to us. We overcame that difficulty and went to the Word of God for confirmations instead of bright lights.

Another example occurred after we had finished starting a number of churches, and I came to a breaking point. The Lord was changing my vocation from being a resident pastor and apostle to that of a prophet to the nations (Jeremiah 1:5, 10). I found myself in a very difficult place called *transition* and an article that I read became very helpful in making the change. It became clear that the root difficulty was operating as an apostolic person, where leaving a church that I had planted in order to start a new one was a reoccurring theme.

After helping people, sharing the Word of God together with them, and forming relationships, it is not easy to have to leave and start all over again in some other place. For my wife it sometimes meant getting a brand-new identity with each new setting. There are times you just don't want the hurt again. I also understand that this occurs in people who get misunderstood or rejected in churches.

I experienced this most recently when, after almost fifty years planting churches and having that become my identity, God said that it was going to change. This was very hard. One night after coming home from The Gate Church, the Lord said, "I want to speak to you. Turn to Proverbs 31:2." I was afraid because that is the godly woman chapter, so I assumed that I must have done something wrong to my wife and I was going to be disciplined. To my surprise, that Scripture is talking about the king's mother, her son in her womb and her vow. God reminded me of my mother's vow to God about having a son and giving him to the world.

God spoke to me and said, "I am executing the vow that Cora Bruhn Herzog made to me as a young girl. Resign from your church, stop starting churches like you have in the past, and be a businessman for Me." I cried for over two hours because I was now having to go another direction and into another unknown. I now have to see myself as a different person as I function in the Body of Christ. However, I still help churches with what experiences and insights I gleaned over the years of doing ministry.

After this period of time, my wife and I did not know where to go or what to do. One of the things that I discovered while visiting churches was that many pastors become insecure when a visitor is equally or more gifted than they are. This made it difficult for us to find a church home. The Lord one day told me to go to a certain church because I was a gift that He was sending there. God wanted me to help but not to pastor that church because He had forbidden me to pastor again in the manner that I used to. That worked for over five years and then one day it became clear that God was removing me as a gift and giving me another assignment. As I left that church, I had a vision of the church in the rearview mirror. I waited on Him for the meaning of the vision, and He showed me that the church in general had lost its influence on the world, but that business had not. Even though this ongoing shift out of the old way of life and ministry was difficult, I learned some important principles about transition, which I have outlined below.

Transition Insights

1. When change happens you have to deal with it because it will not just go away.

2. We need to come into a neutral zone where we process what has happened to us. This is where we have to deal with the hurts and pains of the change.

3. After we work through the neutral zone, we are then ready for new beginnings.

There are many people who are going through this process but do not understand what has happened to them. I have met people who are missing something and feel a yearning for something more, but do not know where to find it.

It was in this context that I had a vision of people who used to be in the game but were now sitting in the bleachers. The Lord told me to get them back into the game. I then began to start clubs that met monthly in order to not get into competition with any churches. As the number of clubs grew, we began to have a different club for every week of the month, and we shared with those who were no longer involved in any church. These clubs lasted for several years, and we still have one that has lasted about six years.

Chapter Eleven
How Could You Be Dumb Enough to Do That?

You would think that I would have learned my lesson about hearing from God, but I apparently needed a refresher course. This time it was about an investment. After two years it became clear that it was a scam, but not until I shared this wonderful investment with a number of our friends. I told them to pray and get the mind of God for themselves. Initially, things seemed to be working, and people were being paid small amounts. Eventually however, I found out that it was a house of cards, and I ended up disappointing many people. After several years of a lawsuit and the loss of many friends, we paid back any funds that we got from it and still hope to finish paying back people who trusted us. I have written a piece about deception which I am including here.

MY ARTICLE ON DECEPTION

There are many forms of deception that influence people. Time has shown us biblical deceptions which we call error or false teaching. In business deceptions, people lose large sums of money through either fraudulent investments or through the exploitation of misplaced trust. We discover that the enemy of our soul is a master of deception and is noted for his deceptive acts in the Garden of Eden.

I am sure that Adam did not think that he was being deceived at the time of eating the apple from his wife. When deception takes root in one's soul, it is an extremely hard paradigm to change or break. Jeremiah 17:9-10 clearly shows us that the heart of man is deceptive at its core, and unless the Holy Spirit intervenes, we are locked into something we cannot get out of. The Scriptures tell us that a hard heart comes from the deceitfulness of sin. That hardness of heart causes one to either become independent out of one's soul strength or corrupt because of sin having its destructive way in that person's life.

I have discovered that deception forms a paradigm, and once accepted, it then becomes solidified as a general truth. From there, you end up allowing it as a general concept in the foundation of your way of living your life. A paradigm of deception is like any other paradigm. It operates on a basic concept, has rules that govern it, and the practice of those rules becomes your way of life. As long as you remain in that paradigm, you are closed off to the truth that many others may see— but you cannot—because of the rules or mental rationalizations that you accepted that formed your paradigm.

This situation became a very painful process in my own life. If God had not arranged a paradigm shift for me, I would still be in that deception. There are basically three kinds of paradigm shifts that can occur in a person's life. The first is when the deception or untruth finally comes crashing down on a person. This is a tremendous blow and can feel hard to believe. That individual was so sure that what he or she did was right, and in some cases, that it was from God. This shift comes in a slow process, but people do not recognize it because—you guessed it—they were deceived. The breaking of the deception comes when the reality of the circumstances and the pain that it is causing become greater than one's rationalization for doing what one was doing. Then comes the devastation and anger along with self-hatred for being so foolish and stupid to become involved in that situation. Later I will explain how one can come out of a terrible situation like I just described.

The second paradigm shift out of deception occurs when a deceived individual encounters someone walking in the truth and desires to experience the same benefits. When this occurs, the deceived individual is brought to a fork in the road and has to choose whether to hold on to the old paradigm or exchange it in favor of the desired benefits. This is particularly true in spiritual deception such as false doctrine or a premise that is not biblically sound or scripturally based.

The third paradigm shift occurs when God sovereignly intervenes in the deceived individual's life through the agency of the Holy Spirit, permanently changing that person. In this case, the deceived individual finally sees his or her identity differently, which then changes how that person views God. This change has the spiritual effect of 2 Corinthians 5:17, which speaks about old things being passed away and all things becoming new.

I would like to try to describe how a person falls into these kinds of deceptions. First and foremost, we have an enemy who sets snares for anyone that can be caught by his trap. In 2 Timothy 2:22-24, Paul describes to Timothy a four-step slide down into the "snare of the devil" type of trap. Research this Scripture passage for personal study, as I did. What causes someone to be deceived often comes out of the personality of the individual.

The first type of deception-prone individual is the strong-willed person as described in 2 Peter 2:10. Strong-willed people tend to latch on to something that they believe (even if it has spiritual connotations to it) and are convinced that they are doing it for God. The Lord may have actually given it to them, but they try to bring it to pass out of the strength of their personality. Often the thought process goes something like this: *If no one else will do it, then I will!* This dependence on their will or strength is what opens them up to the deception. The enemy is ready to supply self-centered ideas and rationalizations to take people out of God's ability and into their own.

Another type of individual who is susceptible to deception is one whose soul is full of fleshly desires, as described in 2 Timothy 3:1-4, 13 and 2 Timothy 2:13. Fleshly desires will lead individuals to believe almost anything—as long as it will help them accomplish their desires—regardless of whether it is for God or just for themselves.

The third opening for deception is putting one's trust in a deceptive or a deceived person. It may not be you who were deceived but maybe the person whom you have come to trust was, and perhaps they put misplaced trust in another individual. This can cause a whole chain reaction of deceptive concepts, ideas or even business policies. In this case, regardless of who caused the deception, the result is pretty much the same. Hebrews 13:7 challenges us to be very careful about whom we trust and gives the basis by which to evaluate who can be trusted.

After gaining these insights, what have I learned out of this whole situation in my life? My conclusion is very simple: be led by the Spirit of God and find trustworthy people to be accountable to. These people can help discern and protect not only our lives but also those of others that we carry responsibility for before God.

Chapter Twelve
Learning to Enter into Intercession

I was introduced to intercession through my wife, Charlotte, who became a part of a women's prayer network called Lydia Fellowship in 1980. The main people involved were the Alpine family out of Washington D.C. Charlotte wanted to get involved in seeing people's lives changed through intercession. I was very apprehensive about letting her get involved, because I thought it would take her away from what I was doing in establishing churches. Due to her involvement, I was invited to be a spiritual advisor. Over time, she became a coordinator for the State of Minnesota and eventually she even became a coordinator for the national board of the United States.

As a result of this involvement, I began to look into what intercession was all about because I was now an advisor. A key Scripture that came to me was Ezekiel 22:30, in which God says, "I am looking for someone to stand in the gap so that I do not have to bring judgement on people." But the Scripture says that because He did not find any, His righteousness and justice required judgment. That

Scripture challenged me to be one that would stand in the gap for other people. I have been doing that ever since.

About twenty years ago, the Lord spoke to me out of Jeremiah 23:18, 22. It outlines coming into the council of the Lord, allowing us to have God's wisdom and knowing what He is going to do. From this position, we can have God alter, through our prayers, people's behavior patterns. As a result, we have had intercession almost every week for the last twenty years, and we have seen miracle after miracle of God changing people's lives.

One of the most evident miracles centered on a young boy in Europe. The problem was that he was going to school and inappropriately exposing himself to little girls. The parents, who were friends of our daughter, asked if we would pray for that situation because they could lose custody of their son if something didn't change.

After prayer, the young boy was delivered from the demons that were harassing him and causing him to expose himself. Within a week he was completely set free, and when he went back to school, his teacher said that he grew up overnight!

However, shortly thereafter, the teacher called the parents and said, "You've got to make your boy stop telling all the children that Jesus came into his heart and that demons left him."

The mother very wisely asked, "Would you like him the way he was before, or how he is now?"

After that, there were no more phone calls from the school. In her travels, my wife has visited this family, personally observing the change in the young boy, and verifying the breakthrough that came from the intercession.

Over the years, the Holy Spirit has taught us several important principles regarding intercession which I would like to outline:

First, we need to operate in the right wisdom, which is expressed in James 3:15-17. Many people mistake natural and earthly wisdom for spiritual wisdom, and then they wonder why their prayers don't get answered! We find in Isaiah 55:6-11 that our thoughts are not God's thoughts, nor are our ways His ways. Prayers do not get answered unless they conform to His thoughts and His ways.

Second, we are invited to come into the heavenly places in Christ Jesus (Ephesians 1:21-22). Our authorization to do so is found in Ephesians 2:6. I discovered in Ephesians 1:21 that there are four types of demonic levels. By exercising our authority and the jurisdiction that comes by having passed through God-given tests, we must bypass each demonic level. What we have found is that each level requires particular weaponry in order to defeat it, and as we gain victory in these areas, we then are able to execute God's purposes through our intercessory prayers. For example, we find strongholds mentioned in 2 Corinthians 10:3-6, which tells us that for every stronghold there is weaponry given by God to overcome it.

Let's look at a real-life example that shows us different jurisdictions. When my wife Charlotte drove our car to a meeting, she prayed and asked the Lord to protect the car and to put angels all around it. On the way, she had an interesting experience that she described this way:

"I was going to take a shortcut to a meeting, when all of a sudden I heard this helicopter directly overhead: it was really close! The longer I listened, the more I realized it was not a helicopter at all—it was my front tire—flopping as noisily as a helicopter!"

She had to call AAA to come change the tire and she went on her way.

About five days later, she started to hear another helicopter noise, and of course, it was the other front tire. I had ordered a new tire, but it had not come in yet, so she was still driving on the spare. Since there was now no additional spare, AAA had to haul the car and her, back to our house in Northfield. Then we had to have another tire put on. This became a crisis for me because two high-quality tires had blown out within the week!

Very kindly, I said, "Honey, pass me the keys to the car; we are not going to drive it any further until we figure out why we keep having flat tires."

Then I began to pray and ask the Lord, "Did this spiritual attack come from Northfield?"

He said, "No."

Then I asked, "Did it come from the county that we live in, Rice County?"

"No."

"Is it from Southern Minnesota?"

"Yes."

"Why, Lord, are we having flat tires?"

He brought back to my mind that I had previously been at a church in Albert Lea, and I had prayed against a local demonic witchcraft coven. I then asked, "Lord, how am I to pray?"

He said, "Bind that demonic realm of Southern Minnesota which is retaliating against you for praying against the witches' coven." I then broke the curse and we have not had a flat tire since.

My wife later asked, "Why didn't my prayers work, but yours did?"

I said, "You lack jurisdiction and authority over the Southern Minnesota demonic realm. I received that authority by ministering at the church and defeating the demonic realm over the area when I was there last."

Anyone is able to have authority and jurisdiction once they have passed through certain demonic realms using the spiritual weapons for that particular spiritual arena.

A third facet of intercession is learning how to cooperate with God's angels. As we discover in Hebrews 1:13-14, angels are ministering spirits that render service to those who will inherit salvation. I discovered that salvation has many facets to it—it is not just going to heaven.

Dennis Miller (a good friend of mine who has gone to be with the Lord) was interceding for me one night after I was attacked by a

84

demonic realm. After having prayed for a long time, he called me at 11:30 at night and said, "Fred, as I have been praying for you, I sense that you need to have an archangel deliver you from this warfare, just like Daniel needed Michael the archangel to help him in his situation."

This is referenced in the tenth chapter of the book of Daniel. Here we discover there are various demonic princes over countries and over kingdoms. As we move in the Spirit, sometimes we encounter these demonic realms.

An example of this occurred when a young man approached me saying, "Fred, please pray for me! I have been sick for the last eighteen months. I have gone to doctors, and I have been prayed for by my friends and my church, but I am unable to get well."

My response to him was, "Let me go into the heavenlies and ask the Holy Spirit for the answer."

After God showed me what the issue was, I told the young man, "You have encountered a demonic fallen angel that you did not have authority or jurisdiction for."

He said, "This is true! I was in Guatemala leading people to Christ and praying for healing, and I do remember bumping into something that seemed stronger than I was."

I proceeded to described to him what it is like to have a fallen angel attack you and what the symptoms are that go with that kind of encounter. A few of them are having extreme weakness, having no energy, feeling like you'll never accomplish anything in life, etc. He told me had all of the described symptoms. I went into the heavenlies and asked the Lord what was next, and I asked Him what weaponry was needed. He showed me repentance was needed, that the authority of Jesus' name must be incorporated, and that there was need of angelic help in this circumstance. As I prayed, the Lord named the archangel that was to help us, so I asked Him to release that angel to accomplish His purposes. Within fifteen minutes, all of the young man's symptoms left, and he has been healed ever since.

A fourth key to intercession came when I discovered that there are various courts in heaven, and that if you want the right answer, you must go to the right court to address your circumstance. I frequent the council of the Lord, as I have described before. It is there that I receive insight regarding Satan's strategy for a given person or situation as well as God's antidotal plan that will bring freedom. This is illustrated in 1 Corinthians 2:6-8, where Satan's plan is overruled by the wisdom of God. I would like to suggest that to the best of my knowledge, there are seven courts which operate in the heavenly realms.

The Courts in the Heavenly Arenas

1. Court of Heaven – Where demonic offenses are resolved
    Zechariah 3:1-7

2. Throne of Grace – Where the legal High Priest intercedes for us
    Hebrews 4:16

3. World Court of Heaven – Where God and Satan trade people
    Job 1:6-12; Isaiah 43:1-5; Ezekiel 28:16, 29:17-20

4. Council of Heaven – Where plans are set
    Jeremiah 23:18, 22; 1 Kings 22:19-23

5. Judgment Seat of Christ – Where believers are judged
    2 Corinthians 5:10; Romans 14:10

6. Great White Throne – Where unbelievers are judged
    Revelation 7:9; 20:11, 12

7. Believers Court – Where believers judge angels
    1 Corinthians 6:2, 3; Jude 6; Revelation 20:4

Each of these courts represents a certain solution for the believer as you understand how to intercede as Jesus is interceding for us.

In conclusion, we need to understand that the enemy of our soul and the enemy of God's plans will retaliate. So, we must learn how to deal with the retaliation. How do we respond when we find ourselves under demonic attack? The pattern that has worked best for me is to ask five questions:

How to Respond When a Demonic Attack Occurs

1. What were you doing before the attack?

2. Where is the attack coming from?

3. What is its jurisdiction?

4. What weaponry is to be used to overcome the attack?

5. What help do you need to overcome the attack?

As I follow those five steps, I find that I am able to free myself from whatever the enemy is forging against me. Here are some additional insights that may be helpful for you, the reader:

How to Have Warfare Freedom from the Enemy

1. Discover what weakness the enemy is using against you

2. Find out what the source in the attack is allowing the enemy

3. Understand the jurisdiction that is involved

4. Find the solution by listening to the Holy Spirit

If you want to break down strongholds, I would make the following suggestions:

How to Break Down Strongholds

1. Recognize what arena you are involved in such as the flesh or the spirit realm– 1 Corinthians 2:14; 1 Peter 2:11

2. Know the facts of the warfare that is involved.

3. Find out what part of the soul the stronghold is located in (i.e., mind, will, or emotions)

4. Expect to execute Biblical weaponry on fleshly areas and bring them into obedience to Christ – 2 Peter 2:7-11 – Lot and his rescue

5. The purpose is to have complete dominance and control in Christ over every stronghold that has been established by the enemy's dominion of the past – Acts 26:16-18 – Paul's call and ministry from Christ

Every person is different, and God speaks to us each in different ways according to our calling, how He has created us, and the vision He has invested in us to accomplish.

Chapter Thirteen
Experiencing Supernatural Relationships

HOW I MET CHARLOTTE – Do you want to go claim souls with me?

I went to North Park Seminary in the fall of 1965 in Chicago, IL. Going to seminary was going to be different for me because I had been in the habit of leading a person to Christ each day. The seminary culture of the time was centered more on the piety of the church than on the salvation of unbelievers.

I soon discovered that I did not fit very well in this cultural setting of academics. But as things would have it, I met some students who wanted to tell me about God and speaking in tongues. One of the students was Sharon Case and the other was her boyfriend, Scott. At this point, I was not interested in speaking in tongues because I had already experienced dreams and visions—that was enough for me. My answer to them was, "You can speak in tongues, and I will have visions." After that discussion the previous night, I saw Sharon again as

I was walking across campus. As she approached me, I began speaking to her about our conversation from the night before. To my astonishment, she said, "I'm not Sharon!" As it turned out, Sharon had a twin sister named Charlotte, a very attractive and outgoing person.

That was our first meeting, and I began thinking, *How can I get to talk to her more?* One evening while at the library, I saw her studying by herself, so I invited myself to sit by her. When the library was about to close, I had to think of something quick, and the only thing that came to me was, "Do you want to go claim souls for God?"

Her answer was, "I have gone out for coffee, and I have gone out for pizza, but I have never gone out to claim souls!"

She was very gracious to me and decided to go prayer walking for souls. That was the divine and supernatural beginning of our relationship. We even laid a fleece before the Lord, that if He wanted us to get to know each other better, that we would see each other every day on campus, and we did. We got engaged, and we married on July 2, 1966.

HOW I MET DENNIS MILLER – Do you want to meet a man who hears from God?

I met Dennis through a friend of his called Bob, who attended a 7:00 AM men's Bible study and discussion at a local bar in the city of Bloomington. The first time a man would come, they would give him ten minutes to introduce himself to the group of businessmen. So, I spoke about the supernatural experiences I was having at a church I was planting in the city of Minneapolis, MN. I shared about God speaking to me as well as the resulting conversions and deliverances of people.

That week, Bob called Dennis and asked him if he wanted to meet a man who hears from God. This initial meeting was very impactful for Dennis, and he decided that I was a key to the breakthrough of a

90

business group that he was a part of that wanted to do exploits for the Kingdom of God. At the same time, my wife Charlotte had been praying for God to give me friends. This was the beginning of a very deep and meaningful relationship with Dennis Miller. He and I meet twice a week for many years and shared deep things on our hearts with each other. He became a very dear friend and fellow visionary, which suited each of us very well. He has since gone home to be with the Lord. He meant so much to me that I have included a poem about our relationship at the end of this book.

HOW I MET JIM GARTLEY – Through God healing his wife, who thought she would die

My wife and I were having brunch with Fred and Avis Somers (close friends of ours) in the Kings Room at St. Olaf College one Sunday after church. When we were just about finished eating, Alexis, a friend of my wife's, came to our table and asked if I would be willing to pray for her friend who was dying that week.

I told her, "Bring her over, and I will pull the dagger of death out of her back, and she will not die!"

Once the friend came over and introduced herself, I asked if I could pray for her, and she agreed. I prayed and realized that the dagger in her back came from intercession for others. After the prayer, she felt the demonic spirit of infirmity leave her body, and she was restored to life at that moment. I mentioned that it would be good if we could meet again and follow up on her condition.

My wife and I met her at a coffee shop near her home, and out of that time developed a regular group that we called a club. She later began hosting this club with her husband Jim at their house. We have now been meeting once a month for the past several years. Out of this relationship, Jim and I have become good friends as well as business associates.

HOW I MET DALE WITHERINGTON – Have you signed your lease yet?

I met Dale and his wife Sue at a pastors' appreciation lunch. Once the meeting was over, I stopped in the bathroom while my wife went on ahead of me. After leaving the bathroom and walking down the hallway, I saw Charlotte talking to a couple that she seemed to know. My wife can talk to anyone, anywhere, at any time. However, these people that she seemed to know were different than the usual strangers that she talks to.

As I came up to them, I heard the number 100,000 in my Spirit. I asked the man (named Dale) if it meant anything to him. That word really got his attention. He said that he had just received a foreign currency bill in that denomination! I also received words that spoke to his wife Sue about her life. After that meeting, we decided to get together as couples, and they shared that they were house-sitting until a house was sold. They were in an in-between time of house-sitting and had to move to another location. Dale shared that they were going to look at another place to live.

As Charlotte and I were driving in the car, I suddenly felt urged to call Dale and ask if they had signed the lease yet.

He responded, "No, we have not yet, but we are on the way to do so."

I was driving the car and spontaneously said to him, "Well, you can come and live with us for a time."

Then I turned to Charlotte and asked, "Is that O.K. with you?" She was in agreement, and we spent the next eight months living together at our house, until the Lord gave us a mutual release. Out of that amazing beginning, we have developed a wonderful and deeply meaningful relationship together. Dale has become a wonderful friend and business associate.

HOW I MET ELENA MAYRHOFER – Are you looking for a husband?

One Spring afternoon, Charlotte, Dale, Sue, and I were sitting outside at the Hideaway Coffee shop in Northfield, MN, when a long-time friend named Heidi came walking by. As she and Charlotte were talking together, a friend of Heidi's walked over who was in her early 20s.

They talked and Heidi said, "Let me introduce you to my friends Charlotte and Fred."

She added, "This is Elena, a friend of mine."

Well, a question came to me from the Holy Spirit, so I asked her if she was looking for a husband! She looked at her friend with an expression that said, *What do I say to him?*

Heidi said, "Go ahead and answer him, because he is a prophet."

When Elena confirmed that yes, she was, I told her, "I train young men and I have one for you!" Well, with that ending she and Heidi went on down the street. My wife gasped and said, "Honey! What are you doing and why did you say that to her?"

About two months later, Elena showed up at the church where I was serving and sat down in the very row that we were sitting in. Sue recognized her right away, and I asked Elena if she remembered what I had said to her on the street. She remembered. I told her, "He is sitting down in the sixth row. Would you like to go meet him?" When she confirmed that she did, we went down before church started and I introduced them to each other.

The end of the story is that they dated and felt that it was the Lord's will to get engaged. They are now married and are a part of our house group on Saturday nights. We have developed a deep mentoring-type relationship, and it has grown into a strong friendship as well.

HOW I MET TIM LUTHER – The numbers are the same!

I met Tim Luther in a very unusual way for men to meet. I had been involved in discipling a young man named Brant and he wanted to take the next step in following a ministry path. I told him that he now needed to start his own group in order to learn how to lead and develop his skills in ministry. That Sunday afternoon, he went back to his hometown and shared Christ at a church party.

I was told that he tried to share with people who were drinking and eating and were not interested in wanting to talk about Jesus. But one guy was willing to listen. He said to Brant, "Come by my office in the morning. I would like to speak with you more." He did, and led that man named Tim to Christ. They got to know each other better, and Tim eventually invited Brant to come and share at his business.

After knowing him for a while, Tim asked, "Being a young man, where did you get all this insight?" Brant replied that it came from being mentored and discipled by a man named Fred Herzog.

Tim's response was, "When do I get to meet this Fred Herzog?" The time was set, and we met at his business. Over time, we got to know each other better. We started by doing some family counseling, which led to his in-laws receiving Christ. After such a positive experience within his family's relationships, Tim said, "If God can do this with my family, what could He do with my business?" This led to my becoming a business consultant in many aspects of his business.

As I was having my time with the Lord one morning, God gave me some unexpected instructions to share with Tim that day. He told me the exact dollar amount that Tim was going to earn that year, and—to my embarrassment—directed me to tell Tim to give me a portion of that amount! My response to God was that this would be a great way to be thrown out of someone's office.

After the business meeting that day, I asked if I could see Tim alone in his office.

He said, "Sure let's go."

With fear and trembling, I read what God had told me. Tim got up, went into another room, and came back talking to himself.

He said, "I can't believe the numbers are the same!"

The number that I had given Tim matched exactly what God had spoken to him the week before.

That began a relationship that lasted for several years and ended in a retainer. Recently, while I was at his dad's funeral, I had a surprising encounter. Several men who Tim had trained came to me and honored me by wanting to meet the man who trained Tim. My relationship with Tim, his wife, and their children has been extremely rewarding in Christ to us. As a family, they have been a great blessing to my wife and me in many ways beyond measure.

Epilogue

This has been an exciting opportunity for me to share what living in the ways of the Holy Spirit can produce—by way of character and blessing—in the lives of many others. It is my desire for readers to be encouraged in their faith and observe what God can do in the life of a simple person who wants to be a servant of God. I have left out many examples because I did not want to expose any particular person or family by sharing intimate details of their lives.

I hope that this has been a book where one can see the underlying principles of how God chooses to act and how He accomplishes His wonderful works. Many years ago, I began to recognize a principle of how God acted in the lives of several of the Bible characters that we call great men and women of God. The first Scripture that spoke to me was when God reveals His relationship with Moses in Psalms 103:7. Here, God shows the distinction between Moses knowing His ways and the people only seeing His acts. The second Scripture is found in Isaiah 55:6-11, where the thoughts and ways of God are clearly described as the avenue by which His word comes to pass.

May this book give glory to God for His wonderful ways. He has provided for, delivered, saved, and revealed His life to us. May this be a challenge to us to bring His personhood and His Kingdom into reality.

A Note from the Editor

I have had the pleasure of personally knowing Fred and Charlotte Herzog for over eight years. I came to Christ two years before I met them at a home group meeting in Burnsville, Minnesota. I was a seventeen-year-old girl who was new in the faith and needed to be discipled, mentored, and cared for. Fred heard that I would be attending North Central University that next fall and introduced me to a student there that he and Charlotte had also mentored.

I began to build a bond with this couple over the years. The Lord has brought deliverance to me and freedom into my life through this couple more times than I could count. They have been spiritual leaders, mentors, friends, and family to me over these past eight years and counting. I am grateful to the Lord for the opportunity to edit the works of Fred Herzog and to see God at work personally in his life and my own.

I would not be who I am today without the Herzog family, and I am eternally grateful that God put these remarkable lovers of Jesus into my life. I love you and your entire family dear Fred and Charlotte, and I cannot wait to see how many more people will be blessed by your lives now through your writings and the Godly lives that you live!

Hannah Vollmuth

My Friend Dennis

Who can find a man to be your friend like Dennis?
You can find him only when He decides to be your friend!
We had coffee almost every week and shared our hearts,
Which carried each of us closer and deeper as men

Dennis is a man who faced death and misunderstandings in life
After meeting his Lord and Savior, Dennis came into his own destiny
A man must face the fear of being a man in order to live as a man
He then gains the integrity of his own soul

I have observed that you no longer stand under the shadow of others,
But you determined to be an overcomer and be a warrior!
You have reached many for the King, whom you have served
And He will say, "Well done, good and faithful servant!"

What a friend you have become to someone in ways so different
And I always think of you as my ready armor bearer
When a man needed a friend, you came to his rescue
You became the answers to many of my wife's prayers

When the battle would rage strong, difficult, and overwhelming
It was you who always became ready to fight and win!
There were so many times that I lost my direction for life,
But I could always depend on you for spiritual insight to set me free

Dennis, I will always be grateful for our many spiritual interchanges
And if you finish first, the other one will be waiting on the other side
This is my tribute to you as a deep friend who always knew God
That friendship has been and is a restoration to many wounded